JUDGE NOT

The Sin and Repercussions of Judging

By Patsy Scott

"The command to judge not is not a requirement to be blind, but rather a plea to be generous. Jesus does not tell us to cease to be men... but to renounce the presumptuous ambition to be God."
John Stott

TABLE OF CONTENTS

FORWARD

Judging is a powerful sin that sets into motion other events, events if given the choice, we would rather not experience. Because it is easy to judge and not know that we are, my hope for this book is that it will reveal and make each of us sensitive to our judging others and bring us to a place where we desperately do not want to judge anyone anymore."

About five years ago, the Lord laid it on my heart to write this book. This came after a good season of the Lord educating me on the subject. In other words, I was given many hands-on lessons regarding judging.

One of those lessons happened when I was part of a ministry team that gave a retreat twice a year. In that retreat I was asked to teach on several subjects, one being *judging*. I felt I had a pretty good understanding of this sin because I had already addressed it in my own life. And, I had addressed it; just not to the degree I soon would be. For in a short time, and in my capacity as a teacher at those retreats, the Lord showed me I yet judged and even suffered repercussions from my judging. I learned that judging affects more than just the moment we make the judgment; it also affects future events.

I hope and pray *Judge Not* will set you free from judging. I pray that a birthing will occur in your heart, a birthing of unconditional love and generous mercy. May you be blessed completely with *Judge Not*.

~ Patsy Scott

When we judge a person, we do so with the false premise
we have all the facts. We do not.

CHAPTER 1

THE SIN OF JUDGING

The *sin* of judging is simply – no, not simply but tragically – making a condemning conclusion about a person, while we think we have all the facts, and the right, to do so. When judging, we actually fence a person in with a negative identity we give them. We pronounce the judgment, be it right or wrong, lacking all good will for the brother or sister we are assessing in our hearts. Why do we judge and what is its root? The root is such things as pride, jealousy and sometimes something as intense as hatred. It flows from our heart as all sin does.

I want to clarify that not all judgments are negative ones. There can be positive judgments. For example: *He is kind*, or *she is truthful*, are positive judgments of someone and is not the same as the sin of judging. The positive judgement does no harm, while the negative does. The one honors a person, while the other dishonors a person.

Every human being is created in God's image, has great significance, and a holy purpose for their life. Because of this, everyone deserves to be given our best. We give them our best by affirming and not negating them, by encouraging and not condemning. Giving our best, we will not judge our brothers and sisters, our friends nor the stranger.

In a court of law, a jury is to judge to the best of their ability, whether someone is guilty or not of a crime. They do this based on the facts they are given. Hopefully, they have all the facts. But, if we are going to judge our fellowman, basically his heart, outside of a court room, we should have all the facts for it to be a just judgment. But we don't have all the facts to a man's heart. Outside of the courtroom, we are not qualified to judge. Nevertheless, we do!

So, what do we base our judgments on if not a full set of facts? Sometimes it is our opinion, sometimes just a feeling. And often it is partial facts that may not be facts at all, but merely a misperception. Judging assumes. It assumes to have all the facts, and the right facts, but doesn't.

When we judge others there is something else that we assume. We assume we have the right to do it. But we do not have this right, and we will never have this right because there is only One who does have the right, and only One who is qualified to judge man. That One is the Lord. He alone possesses all the facts about any one of us. Only God! James 4:12 tells us -

There is only one Lawgiver and Judge, the one who is able to save and destroy. But you—who are you to judge your neighbor?

When we judge, we are playing God. So why do we judge when we are not God and so inadequate for it? Because we have not come to understand the true way of love, that love is kind, forgiving and full of grace.

What does the sin of judging look and sound like so we can identify it when we do it? Remember, judging sizes someone up without *all* the facts, and it arrives at the verdict of guilty. A verdict of guilty condemns the one we judge. Here are a few examples:

- *You idiot!* Someone has just cut you off on the road. You think or say, "You idiot." Is this truth? Is that person an idiot? You don't know the facts to make such conclusion; you only have an experience that lasted 10 seconds. Maybe the driver didn't see you. Maybe it was a new driver, just learning. We don't know and we surely don't know if he or she is an idiot, though we just judged them to be one. This is not a godly way to respond to another human being, though their action may have been reckless and even fatal and even though they probably didn't hear us call them an idiot.

- *Shame on her! She has no discipline!* This is your thought about the extremely obese woman (or man) ahead of you in the checkout lane. You have judged that person because you assume that they are overweight because they lack discipline. You are looking down on them for it. Does she or he lack discipline? Maybe or maybe not; we don't know. But this judgment is condemning and unloving. While judging, we close our heart to the person. Is that what we are to be doing with people who God loves and desires to save? But judging always comes from a heart closed to loving the person we are judging.

- *That man I saw in church last Sunday can't be a Christian. I saw him smoking.* (Or, I saw him at a bar. Or, I saw him drink wine.) This is not the way we are to determine someone's status of salvation. Judging by outward appearances, we ignore the person's heart and even disregard that they have one. This might surprise you, but before it was discovered that tobacco had ill-effects on our health, many esteemed people of God smoked. For example, C. S. Lewis smoked, as did Charles Spurgeon and Jonathan Edwards. * Today, yes, we know it is unwise to smoke because it can shorten our life, potentially causing lung cancer. But smoking has no effect on our salvation nor is it a sign of our lack of salvation. The brother or sister sitting next to us in church may smoke, but we may have too many desserts, or we never exercise. Does this mean we are not saved because we are not caring for our body? What are we to do with all this then? We are to stop judging, and instead love.

- *Mary is always late.* (Implying, Mary lacks in qualities of good character because you have never seen her on time.) This is a matter of looking down on Mary. It is not just stating the fact that she is always late but that we criticize her for it. We have no clue what makes Mary late. Maybe Mary is so often late because her babysitter is late. Or maybe it is that she has seven children to get ready before she leaves the house. But we pronounce Mary always late and check her off as irresponsible because it irritates us. There is surely a better way, a more positive way, to describe Mary. Love offers Mary grace, and even a helping hand, given the opportunity.

- *Tom is an unacceptable Sunday school teacher; I've seen him mowing his yard on Sundays. If he is wrong about that, (working on the Sabbath), he is probably wrong about many things.* This is making a judgment that someone is beneath us because they don't see matters as we see them. The fact is, we can learn something from all people though we may not agree on all things. Sadly, when we make a judgment like this one, we close our spirit to the person, making it impossible to receive anything from them. This is not a case of discerning whether Tom is teaching

11

truth or not. It is a matter of rejecting and judging Tom over a disputable matter and writing him off for it.

Judging is serious. It will stifle relationships, discourage those young in their faith, and break a heart. Scripture warns us of the harmful effects of this sin, that by it we bring trouble. Scripture is also clear that we will be held accountable for all judgments we make, and we have no excuse for judging (Romans 2:1). We need to solemnly heed these warnings.

A spoken judgment pierces the heart of the hearer. And a judgment thought, but not spoken, also has its effect. God hears our thoughts; therefore, a judgmental thought is not overlooked; it is no secret and the Lord will judge us for them. That alone should make us tremble.

Let's consider "thoughts" further. Do they have any effect at all on the one we are judging when they don't even hear it? I would say, yes, they do. I have experienced this personally. I have felt a judgment of me though I did not hear it. It happened this way:

One Sunday morning in church I was having a conversation with the Lord regarding a certain person who I felt I could no longer trust. I wondered why I was feeling this way. I liked this person very much, yet I had an unease with her I could not explain. I prayed, "Lord, show me the source to my feeling this way. Have I done something wrong?"

The answer came to me in a matter of minutes when this person came up to me after church. Our conversation went right to the matter, when my friend admitted she was struggling with me and judging me for something. We had a good and honest talk and resolved our issue; she got clarity and I got released. And there it was, our relationship had been stifled because of a judgment on me I had never heard spoken. I had, however, felt it. Because my friend and I took care of the judgment that day, the unease I had previously felt with her left and did not return.

Wouldn't it be great to clear the air of all the judgments affecting our relationships? Wouldn't it be great if we would be grieved by the sin of judging and cease in it all together? What a good friend she was to come to me and confess her struggle, so we could make all things good again.

Lord, convict us of all judgments we have made and are making. Change our hearts, so that judging would no longer be a part of who we are. Amen.

* C.S Lewis (1898-1963) is the famous author of the *Tales of Narnia*, *Mere Christianity* and *Screwtape Letters* among other books. He was a respected theologian. Charles Spurgeon (1834-1892) was a highly respected preacher called "Prince of Preachers." He died in 1892 but remains highly influential. Jonathan Edwards (1703-1758), an American revivalist preacher, is regarded a great theologian. He is famous for his sermon titled *Sinners in the Hands of an Angry God*.

Every human being is created in God's image and has significance and a holy purpose. Having significance and purpose, our fellowman deserves our best toward him. He deserves our affirming him, not our negating him; he deserves encouragement, not condemnation.

CHAPTER 2

THE JUDGE AND THE JUDGED

When judging occurs, both the judge and the one judged will suffer for it. There are two scriptures to prove this. The first speaks of the judge who suffers being condemned, for he condemns himself. The second, the one judged suffers because he is treated with contempt.

*You, therefore, have no excuse, you who pass judgment on someone else, for at whatever point you judge another, you are **condemning yourself**, because you who pass judgment do the same things.*
Romans 2:1

*You, then, why do you judge your brother or sister? Or why do you treat them with **contempt**?* Romans 14:10a

THE JUDGE
Romans 2:1, the first verse, can't be any clearer. One who judges another condemns himself. To condemn is to doom, curse or sentence. Therefore, when we judge someone, we curse (condemn and sentence) ourselves to commit a sin similar to, or kin to, the sin we judged the person of. *"For you who pass judgment do the same things."* Who is behind the sin the judge will eventually commit? It is none other than the enemy who has just been empowered, and authorized, by the judge to ensnare him so he sins. Let me repeat that. Judging authorizes the devil and his demons to pressure us to sin. This complies with God's law of reaping what we sow.

Six points to remember about the judge:

1. The judge condemns (sentences, curses) himself. (Romans 2:1).
2. The enemy can and will legally ensnare the judge to commit sin. (James 1:15).
3. The judge will eventually commit a sin similar to what he judged (the same thing). (Matthew 7:1-2).
4. The judge is responsible for the curse assigned to himself.

5. The judge is judged by God through experiencing a repercussion for judging. (Romans 14:12).
6. The judge is a stumbling block to the person whom he judges. (discussed later.)

I hope you clearly see that we reap judgment for judgment and that this is a spiritual law set by God.

Do not be deceived, God is not mocked [He will not allow Himself to be ridiculed, nor treated with contempt nor allow His precepts to be scornfully set aside]; for whatever a man sows, this and this only is what he will reap. Galatians 6:7 AMP Bible.

THE JUDGED
When we judge someone, we are treating them with contempt. Contempt is to despise and even hate someone.

You, then, why do you judge your brother or sister? Or why do you treat them with contempt? Romans 14:10a

Treating someone with contempt, we dishonor them in our heart by looking down upon them with our disfavor. How might this contempt feel to them? How might it feel to us? Maybe someone gives us advice but with no empathy. Maybe someone makes a comment like, "You're not *really* going to eat that are you?" How would a statement like that make us feel? Wouldn't we sense the contempt?

To be judged by others does more than just make us feel bad; it can set us up to sin. This is all explained in Romans 14, where a weaker brother is being judged. It says the one passing judgment can be his stumbling block or obstacle.

*Therefore, let us stop passing judgment on one another. Instead, make up your mind not to put any **stumbling block or obstacle in the way** of a brother or sister.* Romans 14:13

An *obstacle* is as a wall or barrier, preventing a person continuing forward. A *stumbling block* causes a fall or a faltering, also preventing or delaying a person going forward. In the context of Romans 14, the obstacle or stumbling block (our judging) interferes with a brother

16

progressing forward in their Christian maturity; realizing a judgment has been cast on him, the weaker brother can cave to our judgment of them and end up doing the very thing they felt was wrong to do. Now they carry guilt for sinning because they saw it as sin.

The one who eats everything must not treat with contempt the one who does not, and the one who does not eat everything must not judge the one who does, for God has accepted them. Romans 14:3

But if you have doubts about whether or not you should eat something, you are sinning if you go ahead and do it. For you are not following your convictions. If you do anything you believe is not right, you are sinning. Romans 14:23 NLT

We are not to judge the person God has not yet convicted to do or believe differently than he does at present. God may be working in this person on the very thing we are judging him for, or He may plan on later working on this issue. We must be patient because when we are intolerant of or impatient with a new believer, we can do them harm.

But we are to be gentle with those new and weak in faith, those yet figuring things out. If we respect them and where they are at, if we honor them and care about them, we will not judge them, making them stumble. Those young in faith are usually very vulnerable. We ought to respect that fact and love them where they are at.

Two points to remember about the person who is being judged:

1. The one being judged will feel contempt coming from the judge.
2. The individual being judged could end up doing something he thinks is sin and bring condemnation upon himself. His walk of faith could suffer a setback.

We see now, scripturally, that judging is destructive to both the judge and the judged. We can only pray - *Forgive us Lord, for all our judging and empowering the enemy to work in our life. Forgive us for the times we judged the weak in faith and caused them to stumble. We take full responsibility for this and ask Your forgiveness. Amen.*

Judging is, as all sin is, destructive.

CHAPTER 3

DOORS

When we judge someone, we open a door to the enemy, allowing him to enter and operate in our life. It is a legal door, meaning he has every right to use it. He whose aim is to kill, steal, and destroy us (John 10:10) can now do that in specific ways; he can put pressure on us to sin, and he can put stumbling blocks for failure at the feet of the one we judged. (Discussed in Chapter 2.) Sadly, these are the repercussions of judging that come through the door we open.

I have a story which describes this perfectly. Yes, it is my story. I tell it because I want you to see that we need to connect the dots and own up to our sin of judging. We need to be aware of the doors we open. This is what happened:

> *It was a Sunday morning and I was in church enjoying wonderful worship and the sweet presence of God. People were answering a call to repent by going to the altar. I noticed someone there who I knew, and I had the thought (yes, just a thought), "Why does ____ (the person's name) keep struggling with the same sin? She goes to the altar almost every Sunday but evidently she isn't getting victory."*

At that moment, I felt I was merely observing. But what do you hear when you read my thoughts above? Do you hear me assuming things? Do you hear condemnation? Do you hear judging? I didn't. I truly thought I was only observing. God, however, did not see it that way because it wasn't that way. I was judging a sister.

In hindsight, we hopefully see what we failed to notice in the present. For me, now looking back, I can see I didn't have true concern for this person's spiritual growth. I didn't hate her and actually thought I loved her, but my heart was not loving her at all because I was judging her – sizing her up with no facts. That Sunday morning, I was in error and didn't have a clue that I was. However, the Lord soon (very soon) showed me I was being a judge that morning.

What was my judgment of the woman at the altar? It was that she had not matured and should have. It was that she ought to be fixed by now and it is her fault she isn't. Shame on her! I wouldn't have said any of this out loud, of course. I knew better. Nevertheless, this my *heart* in the matter; I was having contempt for my sister.

The sin of judging is subtle. I could have missed that I was doing it, and never repented, were it not for the Holy Spirit revealing to me what I had done and showing me how my thoughts were viewed by Father God. You know, we can candy-coat sin, especially when it is a mere thought. And we can deceive ourselves into believing we are not really judging, just thinking. But the Lord wanted me to know thoughts count. So, what happened? He let me feel the ouch of my sin of judging by experiencing its repercussion. Remember, the Word tells us we condemn ourselves when we judge, and it also says we will reap what we sow. The ouch was coming soon - in fact, immediately. The reaping was coming.

First, let's again run over the definition of judging, the part that says we don't possess all the facts. Absolutely, I did not have all the facts about my sister. I didn't even have one fact. All I had was what I was seeing, and believe me, I was not seeing her heart, only an action. I had deemed this poor dear person to be a failure and wrote her off. I had no compassion for her. (I hadn't even thought of going to the altar to pray for her and petition God to make her strong.)

So, here is the ouch part of my story -

I, the judge, had a meeting to attend after church that day. In the meeting was an individual I had had a degree of difficulty loving and accepting. I had prayed about this quite a lot and repented but would find myself failing once more in loving him. So, again, I would repent. But presently I felt I had finally gotten victory in this because I had nothing but warm feelings toward this person who I was now with in a meeting.

The meeting began, and I found myself becoming argumentative, even challenging what this particular individual was saying. Clearly aware of the agitation in my heart towards him, I also knew it was the enemy at work and that he had gotten into my thoughts, and worse yet, my words. My heart had gone awry once more with this person, and I had just succumbed heartily to the enemy. As I left that meeting, I knew the devil had just had his day with me.

Heading home, I pondered what had just happened and asked myself, "Why was I failing again with this person?" After some more pondering and when discussing this with my husband, the light of understanding came on and I saw it! I recalled the thoughts I had had toward my sister at the altar that morning, the thought that she couldn't get over her problems. I realized right then that I had judged her for not getting victory and there I was, a few minutes later, not getting my victory either. I think this is called eating humble pie.

My slice of humble pie that day led to my having a revelation. The humbling was my due, but also my blessing. The humble pie I just ate required I do something with my sin of judging and my sin in the meeting.

Repercussions from sin, and reaping what we sow, is reality. Jesus tells us:

Do not judge, or you too will be judged. For in the same way you judge others, you will be judged, and with the same measure you use, it will be measured to you. Matthew 7:1-2

The same measure? That is the ouch. In order to learn compassion for others, I needed a similar measure. And so it happened, my repeating a sin I felt I was done with; it got my attention and the Holy Spirit saw that I connected the dots.

REPENTANCE
Back to my story - I had judged the person at the altar, I was getting the backlash from it, and I needed to do one more thing. I needed to repent. This I did, praying to God and asking His forgiveness. I broke the power of the judgment over myself and the one I judged, and I broke my agreement with the enemy. (When we sin, we go into partnership, by agreement, with the enemy.) I went further and spoke to my friend from the meeting, asking his forgiveness. I had to do this and could not let it go. It was humbling to say the least, but with repentance and action, I took back from the enemy the right I had given him to inflame the

21

atmosphere in my relationships.

How many times do we judge but are not aware of it? How many times do we not recognize we are suffering from a judgment we have made? How many of our troubles are of our own doing and could have been avoided if we had not judged, and thereby, opened a door? Let it be our prayer to ask the Holy Spirit to show us when we judge, so we may repent immediately, receive forgiveness, and break all curses brought on by our judging. In this way, we close the doors we should never had opened in the first place.

FORGIVENESS
Forgiveness is powerful in bringing us back to blessings. First, if we sense someone is judging us, we should obey the Lord's command to forgive them. And when we ourselves judge, we ought to repent and ask forgiveness. We need to seek forgiveness from the one we judged if it was a judgment that we spoke out loud to them, and from God. Further, we need to make sure that we *receive* His forgiveness and also forgive ourselves. Forgiveness, in all directions, is huge. By forgiving and breaking judgments, we can stop the repercussions.

PRAYER
Father, in the name of Jesus Christ, I break all judgments against me. I bind, rebuke and bring to no effect all criticism and condemnation spoken or thought against me. I forgive all who have so judged me or spoken negatively of me. I also repent and receive your forgiveness for judging others. I now appropriate the power of the Cross and the blood of Jesus Christ to stop all demons from carrying out any curse towards me arising from being judged, or towards others, arising from my judging them. I break all assignments to place obstacles or stumbling blocks before me or the ones I judged. I do this in the name of Jesus Christ. Lord, please bless those now whom I have judged and give me greater wisdom and compassion for them. I now receive freedom from the effects of judgments. I ask that all the enemy has stolen from me, be restored and that all be restored to the ones I have judged as well. I ask this in the name of Jesus Christ. Amen.

With godly actions, like repentance and forgiveness, we can again enjoy blessings from the Lord. We can shut the door to the enemy's legal rights and get back to fulfilling our purpose in God – to love Him and to love others.

We need the help of Holy Spirit to connect the
dots from our judging to the repercussions.

CHAPTER 4

GOD'S REDEEMING NATURE

Psalms 103:4 tells us the Lord redeems our life from the pit and crowns us with His love and compassion. When we judge, we definitely step into a pit we need redeemed (released) from. Because it is God's nature to redeem us, he will do what only He can do to purify us from our unrighteousness when we judge (1 John 1:9). And, He gives us wisdom as we experience His wondrous love in this way. I have a friend with a story that well exemplifies that God desires we reap the blessing of learning from our mistakes. This is Alice's (fictitious name) personal experience with God's redeeming nature.

> *My mother-in-law was going through a difficult time of depression and required daily assistance so she would follow her hygiene and eat meals. My sister-in-law (her daughter) had helped for a while but then stepped back and said, "No more." I knew my mother-in-law had not been an ideal mother, maybe even toxic, in the raising of her children. However, I felt my sister-in-law's patience could have been better; I felt she should have been able to extend some extra grace to her mother in the present circumstances. I could not understand why she didn't have more compassion. More than once I had faulted her, as well as my husband, for this.*

> *With my sister-in-law's stepping back, I was the one expected to jump in and pick up the daily monitoring and assisting of my mother-in-law. I rather enjoyed it, pleased to have opportunity to speak to her about faith and to love on her. We were getting along quite well - that first week.*

> *In week two, in my quiet time and unrelated to my duties with my mother-in-law, I had prayed a covering prayer in which was the phrase, "I break all judgments I have made." It was a general breaking of judgments, not specific. To be truthful, I wasn't conscious of any judgments I was making at the present and had prayed only to cover myself in case I had. I sincerely believe, because of that prayer, wheels started turning, because the repercussions for judging my sister-in-law and husband came to*

the forefront like a flash. I believe God allowed this, that I might repent specifically and learn some things.

What happened was my mother-in-law, with whom I thought I was bonding, lashed out against me. In a quiet, but accusing voice, she criticized something I had just done. I had sat down at a piano in the common room of the nursing home, which was not occupied at the time, and picked at the keys. She accused me of overstepping my boundaries, and her scorn of me was impossible to miss. I saw an evil presence in her eyes that day, manifesting a spirit that had been hidden from me in the past. It was clearly malicious. At first, I didn't know how to respond or how to handle this. Sadly. I didn't think long, my heart just responded with, "No more, I am not coming back."

Upon reflection of this event, it didn't take me long to realize I had done the very thing for which I had judged my sister-in-law for. But now, I understood her; now, I had compassion toward her.

Later, discussing this with my husband who said with a soft chuckle, "Welcome to our world," I came to understand a little better the mother/child issues in my husband's family. Though I had just experienced only a small bit of the toxicity of this troubled woman, I realized what my husband and his sister had suffered in childhood was far greater than my one brief experience. I repented and confessed I had judged these people, my husband and his sister. I also praised God for the new insight and compassion I now had for the offspring of my mother-in-law. There is more to this story, but I will leave it here. The point is, I was shown that God is very much into redeeming His children through the "reaping what we sow" principle. He loves to give us beauty for ashes. God is good, and I now count it all joy when I suffer various trials – like this one!   ~ Alice.

As much as we wish never to judge, we do. With that said, we can rejoice knowing the Lord's hand of correction will cause us to grow, as He brings us to the other side of our sin. This He does by allowing repercussions. If the Father didn't care about us so, He wouldn't do this. But He does care. Our responsibility is to pay careful attention, so we reap something beautiful from our mistakes. As we see in Alice's story, the Lord is for us not against us, and He will cause our failings to be used for good (Romans 8:28) as we humble ourselves before Him. It is His redeeming nature to do so!

I thank the Lord for all blessings that come through the repercussions of sin. Our Lord is a redeemer, not a condemner. When we fail at goodness and righteousness, He will use it, showing us how to be better people. Open to correction, we will receive blessings.

Our Lord redeems us. He does not condemn us,
but loves and teaches us.

CHAPTER 5

GOD'S QUIET VOICE OF CORRECTION

There will be times, when we judge, that we will hear the voice of the Lord quietly correcting us. If we listen to that voice and stop right there, repercussions can be avoided. This is by far the preferred way to deal with our sin of judging. We must, however, be listeners and respecters of the voice of God.

If you have this kind of relationship with the Lord, where you discourse with Him throughout the day, you are familiar with Him speaking into your present situation with truth. Hopefully, we give full attention to His calm voice calling us out on things, so we will avoid the sterner voice required when we don't.

How might a conversation go between us and the Lord when we have just judged someone? Here are some examples. I use the fictitious name Mark.

Example 1: Mark has just mentally chided some young people he observed idly hanging out at the mall. The Lord heard his silent thoughts and said to him –

> *"Mark, you behaved similarly when you were young."*

After a moment of contemplation, Mark replied –

> *"Oh, Lord, I did. I'm so sorry. I am judging them. Forgive me. They are young and I should not be so unloving toward them. I should not have judged."*

Example 2: Mark has just cringed at someone using vulgar language and four-letter words in casual conversation. He finds this person undesirable to spend time with because of this. The Lord's gentle voice says to Mark –

> *"Mark, that man doesn't know Me. Why don't you choose to accept him, love and pray for him? I could transform his heart so that his lips would praise and not curse me. But if you judge him, he will sense your disdain of him, and his heart will*

become as stone toward me."

And Mark's reply was –

"Lord, I am so sorry I judged this man's heart. Of course, this man is worth praying for. You love him as he is, and I should too. Forgive me for viewing him as not worthy of love."

You see how this works? God's gentle voice of correction brings us to repentance immediately. Praise God, He reminds us of our imperfect past as well as our flawed present. He reminds us who we are - forgiven sinners. He leads us to having greater compassion, love and concern for others. With a simple conversation, the Lord will turn us around, so we become extenders of grace and mercy. This conversation with the Lord, is not condemning like the voice of the enemy is when he reminds us of our past, so we feel bad. The Lord is not accusing us, only reminding us we are no different than the one we are looking down on at present.

Christ, who came not to judge but to love us and bring us into the family of God, loved us while we were yet sinners (Romans 5:8). He did not look down on us, but He looked into us, and saw our pain and emptiness. Shouldn't we be as Christ toward all people and stop judging? Shouldn't we love others better, and do so with all our being?

I pray Father, that we Your church would have ears to hear Your gentle voice of correction and allow You to soften our hearts for loving. May we not look down on others, but into others, seeing their heart, and acknowledging you love them. Amen.

The Lord is in charge of all training in righteousness
and the One growing us in love.

CHAPTER 6

APPROPRIATING THE CROSS

Appropriating the Cross is a response of our heart, personally, to the death and resurrection of Jesus Christ. We appropriate by receiving and applying what the work of the Cross gives us. Appropriating may be a new concept to you, and you may think you have never appropriated anything in your life in a biblical way. But if you are a believer in Jesus Christ, you have. You have appropriated the finished work of the Cross, for your salvation.

An appropriation of the Cross can be in a silent whisper of the heart, as well as an audible prayer or proclamation. It is important we realize that it is not only the work of the Cross we are blessed with, but the *finished* work of the Cross. Jesus said in John 19:30, "It is finished." And it is. We need not doubt this ever. And because it is finished, the devil cannot argue our appropriation of it. The power the devil once had over us, has been conquered by the Cross.

> *Since the children have flesh and blood, He too shared in their humanity so that by his death He might break the power of him who holds the power of death—that is, the devil— and free those who all their lives were held in slavery by their fear of death.* Hebrews 2:14-15

Salvation is not the only benefit of the Cross; there are many benefits. For example, access to the Holy Place, the presence of God, is one such benefit. We appropriate this benefit every time we go to the Lord in prayer, believing He hears us. This appropriation is based on the fact that when the physical veil in the temple was torn at the moment of Christ's death, the spiritual veil that had separated us from the Holy Place of God was also torn. Because the work of the Cross is a finished work, that veil remains torn for us, so that all who love God may *always* enter into His presence.

Another benefit of the Cross we can appropriate is the right to break curses in the name of Jesus. This includes the curses brought about by the sin of judging. Because Christ became a curse for us, we have this benefit and authority.

Christ redeemed us from the curse of the law by becoming a curse for us, Galatians 3:13a

The Hebrew word for curse(d) is 'arar. 'Arar means to be without protection. For us, when a curse is in effect in our life, we are out from under God's protection from the enemy in a specific area. But with repentance, and our appropriation of the Cross to break curses, we can come back to being under His umbrella of protection. Thanks be to God for the work of the Cross we can fully rely on. We are wise when we do not let such benefits lay dormant; we are wise to pick them up with appropriation.

When we appropriate the Cross to remove curses, we do the following -

1. **We Believe**

   We *believe* God's Word that says sin brings a curse. We *believe* Jesus forgives us when we confess our sin and repent. We *believe* Jesus took upon Himself all curses, freeing us from them. (Daniel 9:11; 1 John 1:9; Galatians 3:13)

2. **We Take Ownership**

   We take personal *ownership* of this benefit of the Cross which we believe in. Because we believe what Christ did on the Cross was done for each of us, personally, we take it for ourselves. (John 3:16; Romans 6:22)

3. **We Apply**

   We *apply* what we believe and have taken ownership of by speaking with God-granted authority, "In the name of Jesus, I break the curse." (Luke 10:19). We can do this only because of the Cross – Christ's death and resurrection.

4. **We Receive**

   We *receive* freedom from the curse we have broken, because Jesus Christ and His blood have power over the enemy and all curses. (Revelation 12:11). We thank the Lord for this.

When we pray to break curses related to judging, we should be as specific as we possibly can. We should be specific because specific demons are at work. When we do, the enemy will back off as we appropriate with faith, authority and a clean heart.

Here is a very effective prayer for breaking judgments (curses):

> *I ask You to forgive me Lord, for my judgment against* _____
> *that they* _____*. I forgive myself for this judgment.*
> *I now remove all legal rights and power I gave to the demonic*
> *spirits to carry out this judgment (curse). I release God's freedom*
> *and healing to* _____ *(the person we judged). Amen.*

Praise God! This simple prayer will stop the activity of assigned demons because it removes their legal right to go after us, and the one we have judged. If we do not repent in such a way, the devil can, and will, continue operating through the judgment.

After appropriating the Cross to stop judgments (curses), it is our privilege to bless the person we had judged. We can bless them with all that is opposite of what we judged them for. For example, if we had judged someone for not being authentic in their faith because we saw them mowing their yard on a Sunday, we can ask God to bless them as they mow; we can bless them to hear His voice and be touched by His Spirit. We do this in the last fill-in of the prayer above, letting words of blessing come out from our renewed, caring and compassionate heart, meaning every word.

We appropriate the Cross by receiving and applying what it gives us, personally.

CHAPTER 7

WHEN JUDGING IS A FAMILY THING

We all inherit generational curses from our ancestors as a result of sins they committed and did not ask forgiveness for. These are sins that we need to put under the blood of Christ to stop their effect on us. Exodus 20:5 tells us that those who do not obey the Lord (sin), will receive a curse (empowerment to fail) which is then passed down to their descendants to the third and fourth generation.

> *I the Lord thy God am a jealous God, visiting the iniquity of the fathers upon the children unto the third and fourth generation of them that hate me.* Exodus 20:5 KJV

In the Holy Scriptures we see that sins need confessed and repented of not only for the benefit of the individual but for the benefit of generations to come (Exodus 30:10). Unless repented of, the curse from sin has weight. Therefore, if our ancestors did not repent, we need to repent for them to free *ourselves* and later generations from the impact of their sins. This is called *identification repentance.*

> *"'But if they will confess their sins and the sins of their ancestors— their unfaithfulness and their hostility toward me, which made me hostile toward them so that I sent them into the land of their enemies—then when their uncircumcised hearts are humbled and they pay for their sin, I will remember my covenant with Jacob and my covenant with Isaac and my covenant with Abraham, and I will remember the land.* Leviticus 26:40-42

We can pretty well know that generational influence is being visited upon a family line when we see an inclination to commit a same sin reoccurring in multiple generations. This *inner pressure* to commit the sin is called iniquity in the Scriptures. To have an iniquity then, is to have a propensity, inclination and susceptibility toward a sin. It comes to those in the family line randomly. Note, we are not finger pointing nor blaming our ancestors for our own actions. We still have free will to sin or not to sin; we are still fully responsible for our own actions.

To further make the case for generational influences, consider such sins as alcoholism, anger, or adultery that keep occurring in a family's line. "He is just like his father" or, "He is just like his grandfather," we might hear said, alerting us of a possible generational curse at work. (Generational curses are also seen physically, such as cancer and heart conditions being passed down in the generations through DNA.) Haven't you witnessed this yourself in families?

Being influenced by our ancestors is not all doom and gloom, however. There is a brighter side – blessings, which are also passed down - a good sense of humor or a giving and generous spirit are some examples. These we want, of course. But we don't want the curses. Those, we prefer under the blood of Christ. Praise God, repentance for our ancestors' and our own sins, including the sin of judging, breaks the propensity (pressure, pull) in us to judge, making the sin easier to resist. (We must still choose not to judge.)

God sees us as family, and because of that, what happens in the family, even way back, affects the family way forward! In Hebrews 7 we see scriptural proof of this, for it was reckoned to Levi to have paid tithes through his ancestor Abraham, though Levi was born several generations later.

And, as I may so say, Levi also, who receiveth tithes, paid tithes through Abraham, for he was yet in the loins of his father when Melchizadek met Abraham. Hebrews 7:9-10 KJV

This is an example of a generational blessing and is another foundational verse we base the confessing of the sins of our ancestors on. The good news is, because of Jesus' death and the new covenant of His blood, when we confess and repent of the sins of our ancestors, we stop the curse (iniquity and pressure to sin) that came because of them. We can look at this as a completing of a transaction. If an ancestor has himself confessed to God and repented of his sin, then the curse, of course, is broken, and we will not see it continued as a pressure in later generations. But, if we see a propensity still working, we can assume somewhere in our family line, the sin has not been repented of.

If we confess our sins, He is faithful and just to forgive us our sins, and to cleanse us from all unrighteousness." 1 John 1:9

God is a just God, giving blessings to those who obey and love Him, and punishment to those who do not (the unredeemed). Praise God we have forgiveness through Jesus Christ!

> *. . . yet he will by no means leave the guilty unpunished, visiting the iniquity of fathers on the children and on the grandchildren to the third and fourth generations.* Exodus 34: 6-7. NAS

God's character is the same today as it was yesterday; He does not change (Hebrews 13:8) but still weighs sin as He did in the Old Testament. Just look around! It is not hard to see that sin brings trouble and obedience to God brings blessings. But because of Christ's death upon the cross (Galatians 3:13), accompanied with confession and repentance, our descendants are recipients of blessings for thousands of generations. We are disciplined for our sins, but not punished.

> *The Lord, the Lord God, compassionate and gracious, slow to anger and abounding in lovingkindness and truth; who keeps lovingkindness for thousands, who forgives iniquity, transgression and sin.* Exodus 34:6 NAS

If you feel judging is a generational curse in your family line, it would be wise to repent for your ancestors, and yourself, and break the pressure within you to judge. Consider praying this prayer:

PRAYER
Father, I confess the sin of my ancestors, my parents, and my own sin, of judging. I forgive and release them for the sin, the curses and the consequences of this sin in my life. I ask You to forgive me, Lord, for this sin, for yielding to it. On the basis of Your forgiveness, I forgive myself for judging. I renounce the sin and curses of judging. I break its power from my life through the redemptive work of Christ on the Cross. I receive God's freedom from this sin and from the curses. I receive a heart that is merciful, forgiving and compassionate towards others. Amen.

God sees us as family and because He does, what happens in the family, even way back, affects the family, way forward!

CHAPTER 8

SAWDUST AND LOGS

When we have genuine concern for our brother or sister and are willing to be part of any solution for them and their condition, we will not be enticed to judge them; but we will be determined to help them. If we have true concern, we will be gracious to them by offering our support. We will pray for them because we want to see them succeed. The scriptures warn, if we judge, criticize, and condemn, we do not help but actually make things worse. Therefore, we should check our attitude before we address any sin we see in someone else.

> *Do not judge and criticize and condemn [others unfairly with an attitude of self-righteous superiority as though assuming the office of a judge], so that you will not be judged [unfairly]. For just as you [hypocritically] judge others [when you are sinful and unrepentant], so will you be judged; and in accordance with your standard of measure [used to pass out judgment], judgment will be measured to you.* Matthew 7:1-2 AMP

The *Parable of the Sawdust and Log* shows us that we are to be truly concerned for a brother who we realize has sawdust in his eye. The sawdust figuratively refers to a sin, a wrong attitude, or other problem the brother deals with that is a hindrance to his spiritual walk.

When we see a speck of sawdust (a fragment of an offense) in a brother's eye, we should want to address it if this is our friend, because we know that a foreign object in one's eye hinders their vision. So, if we love our friend, we will want to see the sawdust removed so he sees everything clearly.

The parable goes on to speak of not just the sawdust that is but a mere speck, but about logs that are much larger. One is insignificant when compared to the one that is egregious (obvious and glaring).

> *Why do you look at the [insignificant] speck that is in your brother's eye, but do not notice and acknowledge the [egregious] log that is in your own eye? Or how can you say to your brother, 'Let me get*

the speck out of your eye,' when there is a log in your own eye? You hypocrite (play-actor, pretender), first get the log out of your own eye, and then you will see clearly to take the speck out of your brother's eye. Matthew 7:3-5 AMP

Before we attempt to remove even a speck from our friend's eye, there are conditions for us to meet. The first is that we are to make sure, and be careful, that we are not being judgmental. Instead, we are to go to our friend with great humility that comes from our realizing we too are sinners and capable of a far worse sin than the sin we see in them and are concerned for.

Secondly, we must be sure we ourselves are clean; that we have looked at ourselves and repented of any glaring and appalling sin. In other words, we are to be living a godly life the best we can. We must assess our own condition because if we can't see our own sin, we will be tempted to judge our brother for his.

The *Parable of the Sawdust and the Log* makes several points:
- We should never assume the office of a judge.
- All judging by man is done unfairly as we don't have all facts.
- If we judge, we will be judged for it.
- We are all sinners.
- Being a sinner, we are hypocrites to judge someone for sinning.
- Humble before God, repented of our own sins, we can be a help to a brother to repent of his sin.
- Judging is not the way to remove sawdust.

Further on in Matthew 7, we come to verse 6. This verse is very interesting, and we might wonder if it has anything at all to do with the preceding verses (verses 3-5 cited above) regarding judging someone for having sawdust, when we have logs. But it does. Look here at verse 6:

Do not give that which is holy to dogs, and do not throw your pearls before pigs, for they will trample them under their feet, and turn and tear you to pieces. Matthew 7:6 AMP

To paraphrase verse 6 so we see how throwing holy things to the dogs relates to judging, I would put it this way: we should not give what is sacred (our relationships with one another) to the dogs (the devil and demonic powers) because our pearls (right relationships) are heavenly blessings. Therefore, do not judge but be humble when dealing with your brother and sister in the Lord regarding his sin.

You see, judging throws a relationship into the hands of the enemy. We are told plainly in Matthew 7, that if we dare to judge when we ourselves are unclean and fail to see that we are, we will be trampled and torn to pieces by the demonic assignment judging invites. How clearer can this be? Let us respect what the parable is telling us and make sure we accurately assess ourselves. Let us not be arrogant but humble enough to see we are sinners and no different than our brothers and be willing to repent of our own sin. Only then can we speak to our brother with genuine concern and without judgment. We will approach him with love, mercy and compassion. With the right attitude, friends can help friends.

We will go to our friend about his sin, with great humility, if we realize we too are sinners and capable of far worse.

CHAPTER 9

THE POWER OF WORDS

Words hold power. In fact, we know that God, with words, brought forth creation. He spoke, and it became so.

By faith we understand that the universe was formed at God's command. Hebrews 11:3a

It is vital we understand the power of *our* words, especially in the matter of judging. It is vital we know that the words we sow, negative or positive, reap a negative or positive effect.

Do not be deceived: God cannot be mocked. A man reaps what he sows. Galatians 6:7

Because we reap what we sow, we have the power to reap (bring about) death or life with our words. Which will it be?

Death and Life are in the power of the tongue. Proverbs 18:21

This truth about death and life being produced by our words should never be taken lightly. However, based on the words we choose to speak, we can see that we are often guilty of ignoring this advice. Even our thoughts, which are merely unspoken words, carry the power to bring about good or the bad. God hears our every thought and thus thoughts are not exempt from the law of sowing and reaping. Satan said *in his heart* (meaning, he thought it) that he will rise above God and make himself like God. By his thoughts, Satan was condemned – banished from heaven. We cannot argue then that even thoughts sow life or death.

You said in your heart, "I will ascend to the heavens; I will raise my throne above the stars of God; I will sit enthroned on the mount of assembly, on the utmost heights of Mount Zaphon. I will ascend above the tops of the clouds; I will make myself like the Most High." But you are brought down to the realm of the dead, to the depths of the pit. Isaiah 14:13-15

Words are powerful to bless (Proverbs 13:3), or powerful to ensnare and trap (Proverbs 6:2). They will either free us or condemn us:

> *But I tell you that everyone will have to give account on the day of judgment for every empty word they have spoken. For by your words you will be acquitted, and by your words you will be condemned.* Matthew 12:36-37

We will answer to God for our words, not excluding those that are idle (pointless) and empty (without meaning). Guard our mouth, we are warned, because words either acquit (clear, release) or condemn (doom) us.

What do we do with this? We learn to speak wisely, and we also learn to recognize the spirit behind our words. We do this so that when they are not in line with God's thoughts, we will reject them and speak the opposite. We can filter all our words through the Holy Spirit and the Word of God. Jesus did this. In John 8:26 He spoke of hearing first from the Father and then speaking. And in John 8:28, He tells us he speaks only what the Father has taught him to speak. Taught Him! We too can be taught. This is up to us. Will we speak life and truth, advancing the kingdom of God, or will we speak death and judgment, advancing the kingdom of Satan?

> *With our mouth we can either bless or curse.* James 3:10

Though Satan often tries to infect our words, we do not have to succumb to his schemes. We can walk in the Spirit by listening to the Father as Jesus listened. And, we can guard our mouth by putting a tight rein on it (James 1:26). We should want to manage our words and refrain from judging because if we don't, our words can be as fire bringing certain disaster.

> *The tongue is a fire, a world of evil among the parts of the body. It corrupts the whole body, sets the whole course of one's life on fire, and is itself set on fire by hell.* James 3:6

May our words not be fire from hell, but living water from the Lord to refresh others.

"Those who judge, will never understand. And those who understand, will never judge." Anonymous

CHAPTER 10

THE POWER OF AGREEMENT

To agree with someone about anything is powerful. The enemy knows this and therefore tries to divide and separate us through disagreements. He much prefers, if we are to agree, it would be with him. And we do sometimes agree with the devil. We agree with him whenever we sin. Therefore, when our sin is judging, we are agreeing with the devil to accuse our brother. Satan, after all, is the accuser of the brethren (Revelation 12:10).

Might we grasp the seriousness of partnering (agreeing) with the enemy when we judge. In the verse below from Isaiah, God makes it clear that when we covenant with the devil, we are believing a lie, even trusting in the lie as we would trust in a refuge. This is not something to boast about. Nor should we arrogantly believe that nothing bad will come from it. It will. Isaiah quotes the words of those covenanting with the enemy through agreement:

> You boast, "We have entered into a covenant with death, with the realm of the dead we have made an agreement. When an overwhelming scourge sweeps by, it cannot touch us, for we have made a lie our refuge and falsehood our hiding place." Isaiah 28:15

We should never partner with demons and trust the lie that we will not suffer for judging our brother or sister.

> I do not want you to be participants with demons. You cannot drink the cup of the Lord and the cup of demons too; you cannot have a part in both the Lord's table and the table of demons. 1 Corinthians 10:20-21

When we agree with the enemy, our accuser and our brother's accuser (Revelation 12:10), we are participating in the cup of demons. However, when our agreement is with God *not* to judge our brother but to love him, we remain in God's favor and can participate in His table where we are blessed with open communion with Him.

The power of agreement can be further understood in the story of the Tower of Babel. Here the people made a sinful agreement to put themselves above God by building a tower they felt would be higher than God. God said that when the people act as one (agree), nothing shall be impossible for them. (You can read this account in Genesis 11.) The principle to be learned here is, that for either good or bad, when people agree the possibility of getting what they want is increased. This is a spiritual truth; it can be used for either bad or good. If all our agreements would be godly agreements, if we would agree with God not to judge but to bless, if we would agree with what the Lord says of our brother and not what the devil's accusations say of him, oh the possibilities! This is where we want to be, utilizing the power of agreeing with the Lord by loving our brother and sister with non-judgmental words that bless and lift them up.

Consider this beautiful promise given to us when we agree in prayer:

"Again, truly I tell you that if two of you on earth agree about anything they ask for, it will be done for them by my Father in heaven. Matthew 18:19

The positive power of agreement is witnessed in answered prayer. When we say amen to a brother's prayer because we agree it is the Lord's will, this has impact with God. When we agree with God and encourage rather than judge others, again, this has impact and good things are made possible.

48

We should never trust the lie that we
will not suffer for judging.

CHAPTER 11

UNITY

Unity in the body of Christ is honored by Father God. Disunity, on the other hand, is honored by the devil who is ever busy bringing discord and division, church hurts and church splits. At the root of church hurts and splits, we will often find the sin of judging. Judging should be given no place in the church but bearing with one another and forgiveness should. According to Colossians 3:13-14, the model church is made up of people whose love for the Lord, and for one another, binds them together in unity.

> *Bear with each other and forgive one another if any of you has a grievance against someone. Forgive as the Lord forgave you. And over all these virtues put on love, which binds them all together in perfect unity.* Colossians 3:13-14

How can we who are the church come to such unity if we are judging one another? We cannot. Chapters 14 and 15 of Romans is full of wisdom on this very subject. I invite you to study those chapters in full as I will only point out a few key verses. I feel, if these verses were applied, we would refrain from judging and experience the unity God desires us to have.

First, we need to be accepting of one another, especially those weak in faith.

> *Accept the one whose faith is weak, without quarreling over disputable matters.* Romans 14:1

When we do not accept those weak in faith, we are being cold and insensitive. We ought to accept people in all stages of their Christian walk. When we don't, and we go so far as to even quarrel with them over disputable matters, we are as lions attacking lambs. Disputable matters are unclear matters. They are not to be argued over for this very reason. We ought to refrain from making issue over them, and refrain from inviting division. And we ought to love and accept fully the brother who leans toward a different view than we do. Because we are not all of one mold and one view, we should not hold one another in contempt for seeing things differently. (This is not to say we compromise on the basic truths of the Gospel.)

For God has accepted them. Who are you to judge someone else's servant? To their own master, servants stand or fall. And they will stand, for the Lord is able to make them stand. Romans 14:3c-4

All God's servants will stand, for the Lord will make sure they do. But when we judge a brother, we work against their standing firm; we work against what the Lord is doing in them. Let us stop all judgments, accept our brother, and encourage unity in the body of Christ.

Second, we need to edify one another. Judging will lead us away from peace, but edification leads us to peace.

Let us therefore make every effort to do what leads to peace and to mutual edification. Romans 14:19

Let us train ourselves in edification and make all effort to do that which leads to peace within the church. A church at peace is a healthy church capable of experiencing God deeper; it will be a church that grows. (Ephesians 4:13).

If we will refuse to judge and not be critical of one another, if we will be for and not against our brother, and if we will always extend mercy and grace, then we will know unity. A house divided against itself cannot stand (Mark 3:25) but a house united will.

How do we stop judging and encourage unity within the body of Christ?

- We can resolve to mature in our faith. (Eph. 4:13).
- We can choose to have concern for one other. (I Cor. 12:24-26).
- We can admit we have trials of our own. (I Cor. 12:24-26).
- We can bear with one another and forgive. (Col. 3:13).
- We can live in Christ and allow Christ to live in us. (John 17:23).

If Christ-like in our character, we will have concern for others, bear with one another, and forgive. We will do that which brings unity to the body of Christ. We will not judge.

A house divided against itself cannot stand,
but a house united will.

CHAPTER 12

GIVING TESTIMONY

The ninth commandment tells us to not bear false witness (a testimony that is false) against a brother or sister (Exodus 20:16). A false witness will lie, generating a wrong perception of someone. The good and worthy qualities the person possesses will be disregarded as a result of the lie. When one falsely testifies against someone, they cause that person to be judged based on wrong information.

Sometimes, we will be a "misleading" witness rather than a false one. We don't lie as a false witness does, but we do provide unnecessary information that can destroy a good name. Revealing a negative truth when it is not necessary, shows we lack compassion. Love protects a brother's dignity and self-worth and will not give needless testimony that could lead others to judge our brother. Love preserves a brother's reputation whenever possible.

Example: Someone's name comes up in conversation. We know this person has recently suffered a bankruptcy and so we share that bit of information. But why did we do this? We didn't have even one *good* reason for sharing this fact. But bringing up the bankruptcy implies there is something questionable about the person. Would Christ ever do such a thing as this? Can we even hear Him sharing our personal failings with someone else? I think not. He would only speak well of us so others would think well of us, and not judge us.

We are to have a clear conscience before God and before man (Acts 24:16) that we bear witness only to the truth (John 18:37). What is the truth in the scenario above? The truth is God loves the person who suffered the bankruptcy. He does not cast him off as a failure but cares for his well-being and future. Loving our brother, we will watch what we share about him. We will only bring up his troubles if there is a pure and godly reason to do so. A good name is more precious than riches (Ecclesiastes 7:1) and worth protecting. We can easily rob a man of it when we bear him an injurious testimony, causing others to judge him.

There was a man who had been foolish by delving into witchcraft. Let's call him Matt. Matt eventually repented and returned to church to serve God. But a brother in the church, believing Matt was yet into the occult, spread (testified to) a witness about this, causing others to believe Matt was still into witchcraft. Because of this, Matt was getting blamed for things he didn't do. And those participating in the gossip were beginning to withdraw from Matt and his wife. This couple, unaware of the gossip, could only wonder why this was happening. Eventually Matt heard of the accusations against him, which led him to consider leaving the church. In the end, that is not what happened though. Instead of leaving, Matt and his wife went to prayer. They came against the curse of the judgment created by the false testimony and gave it to God. They were eventually vindicated, and things settled down for them. They are still in that church.

> *Brothers and sisters do not slander one another. Anyone who speaks against a brother or sister or judges them speaks against the law and judges it. When you judge the law, you are not keeping it, but sitting in judgment on it.* James 4:11

When we give a false or destructive testimony, we break God's law of love.

> *For the entire law is fulfilled in keeping this one command: "Love your neighbor as yourself."* Galatians 5:14

May we repent of all gossip, slander, and hurtful testimonies. May we instead choose to bless our brothers and sisters.

We are to have a clear conscience before God and before man that we bear witness only to the truth.

CHAPTER 13

JUDGING OUR CHILDREN

Let's look at specific groups or individuals we tend to judge, beginning with our very own children. Negative words we direct at our young children, especially repeatedly, are actually judgments upon them, condemning them to be that negative thing we proclaim over them. For example, we may rashly say to them that they will never do anything right. Or, we may say to them they aren't smart enough. Words such as these have the power to damage a child for years. Though it is not the parent's intent, they damage their child's identity. Children are extremely vulnerable and will take such words to heart, keeping those words even into adulthood. In adulthood, usually somewhere in mid-life, wounds from judgments can come to the surface affecting many things, but most often relationships.

When a child hears, receives and believes what they are accused of being (you are bad or you will never amount to anything), it is shattering for them. Believe me, I am not emphasizing this enough. I see this again and again in the emotional healing sessions I administer. What the parent will soon forget, the child will not. Having been hurt by words that are not corrected, they sooner or later respond to life according to those words that told them who and what they are. The flawed identity they believe of themselves works against God's identity of them.

You may be thinking you have spoken negative words toward your children, but they seem fine. I hope this is so, but the truth is, negative statements produce inner wounds in children that stay hidden for years, until something happens to expose them.

Christmas was nearly ruined one year for a family when their adult son's hidden wound came to the surface. As Sonja tells it, she was not aware a wound even existed in her son, nor that she was the one who had put it there.

Sonja's married son had posted a picture on Facebook – a picture of himself and a female Sonja didn't know. Sonja's heart was concerned when seeing this picture. It wasn't that she felt her son was being unfaithful to his wife, but she did feel it was inappropriate and imprudent for a married man to post that specific picture. Therefore, Sonja asked her son, "Where was Janice when this picture was taken?" (Janice is her son's wife). Sonja's daughter also posed the same question to her brother, feeling the picture imprudent as well and unaware her mother had the same concerns. Was the picture imprudent? To some yes. But to the son? No. Were Sonja and her daughter judging? Not really, they just wanted clarity, feeling a bit uneasy about the picture. But how did the son react to their comments? He was hurt, he felt judged, and he erupted. Why did he erupt? Why did this hurt him when it shouldn't have? Why didn't he just explain things? It soon came out why, in a conversation between Sonja and her son when he said, "Mom, I am not like Dad!" (A little background here, Sonja was divorced because of infidelity on the part of her ex-husband.)

When Sonja heard her son say, "Mom, I am not like Dad," she immediately remembered words she had spoken to her son many years prior, during the divorce and when her son was a teenager; she had accused him of being like his dad. And now, in the present moment, she saw clearly that what she had spoken long ago was still at work. Twenty plus years later, the effect of her words, words that were a judgment on her son, resurfaced and revealed that his heart was still pierced by them.

Before long all the family was drawn into this emotional misunderstanding. Christmas was approaching, and some of the family wanted to opt out of gathering due to the emotions still not settled. It had always been a close and loving family, but now this.

Can you see in Sonja's story how the devil, some twenty years later, was taking pleasure in his legal ground to destroy a family due to a judgment made years ago on a young man? Sonja will tell you it is too easy to destroy our children with words of judgment. Proverbs 17:27 says a man of knowledge uses words with constraint. I would say this, though we all fail as parents with our words, we should start now taking all words seriously and realize none are insignificant, especially to a child. If we speak wrong words, we can fix them immediately and change our statement. We can ask forgiveness for them. Here is a prayer to break and repent for misused words (judgments):

> *Father, I ask you to forgive me for speaking the judgment against _____ that he/she _____.*
> *I forgive myself for speaking this judgment and I remove all legal rights I gave to the powers of darkness to carry out this judgment. I now release God's freedom and healing to _____ (the person judged). Thank You, Lord. Amen.*

We give powers of darkness access
to our children when we judge our children.

.

CHAPTER 14

JUDGING A SPOUSE

When we complain and criticize a spouse, it is usually in judgment that we do so. I have judged my spouse for not being spiritual enough (according to me, not God), for not being affectionate enough (again, according to me) and for many other things. It was always "not enough." So, what are we doing when we complain that our spouse is not loving us perfectly enough, or not meeting *our* standards? We are judging them for not satisfying our soul. It is only God who can do that. If we can grasp this, we might cease judging our spouse and let them be who they are and appreciate who they are.

Often a husband and wife will be opposites. One may be of a joyful nature, excited about life, fun-loving and pursuing God outwardly as well as inwardly with full engagement. The other may be quiet, reserved and content with very little stimulation (play) in their life and their pursuit of God is private. Two people's stories and how they were raised can be very different, as can be family traditions and the way to discipline the children. These many differences can tempt us to judge the one we vowed to love, honor and cherish. But differences can be accepted and become blessings if we refuse to judge because of them. Actually, differences can give a marriage great balance.

Having unrealistic expectations of a spouse leads to judging them. I know there are valid marital issues to be dealt with, but not through judging. Husbands and wives are to see themselves as a team. A team, given to judging, will falter and fail. But a team will succeed when they cheer each other on in all aspects and not hold unrealistic expectations.

There was one time when I was unhappy with my husband because he was not meeting an expectation of mine. We had a conversation about it, but it did not go well. Probably, because I was judging him. How do I know this? The Lord told me; He rebuked me that night with a dream.

In the dream, I was getting ready for my wedding. I looked at the clock and saw I had only ten minutes to be at the church and walk down the aisle. Ten minutes! I wasn't ready. I was not dressed. I was not bathed. My hair was not done. And my nails were a mess, the polish chipped. I was a mess in every way and not picture perfect like a bride wants to be on her wedding day. I was expected to be radiant in just 10 minutes. But there I was – not.

I began to snap at people in my dream to do this and do that and to help me get ready. But ten minutes to fix all this? It was impossible, and I knew it. And I knew, too, that something had to give, because I was not going to be the perfect bride I wanted to be. I knew that I would have to show up less than perfect. Yes, less than perfect at my wedding! I settled – no bath, but clean undergarments. No new nail polish but the old was removed.

You may laugh, and I agree it was a humorous dream, but it showed me exactly what I needed to see. It showed me that I was the sinner the evening before, and by my judgments and accusations I had brought pain and hurt to my husband (sigh). It also showed me I had no right to expect my husband to be perfect when I am not. I, the imperfect bride, had judged the man of my heart for being imperfect. Who of us are perfect? None. I repented and asked my husband's forgiveness.

How are we to live with the imperfect spouse God has given us? Constructively rather than destructively. With love not judgments. If there are concerns, we address them humbly and look for ways to improve our marriage together. And most definitely we pray, letting the Lord do what He does better than we could ever do; we let him tend to the business of perfecting our spouse in His perfect timing – as well as perfecting us.

If I were to have a conversation with the Lord about this now, it might go a little like this:

"Lord, You promised me a beautiful marriage. In the past, I looked and looked for You to give me that, but I felt You let me down. I often reminded You that You promised it, and that I didn't understand why this promise hadn't been kept. But I must ask You to forgive me, for now I hear what You are saying. You are saying, 'Yes, I promised you a beautiful marriage, daughter, and you have it. You have failed to see that it is beautiful. You

have failed in this because you have focused on that which is imperfect. A marriage can be imperfect and yet beautiful. This is what I want you to see!'

Thank You, Lord. I now see it."

My dream, and the resulting revelation, transformed my attitude toward my marriage and my husband. In the past, I had expected perfect. But perfect can never be, because two imperfect people can only make an imperfect marriage. But beautiful is possible, and I had missed it. I had been blind and unthankful. The unbathed, unpolished, and quite messy bride was rebuked and shown she was in a beautiful marriage with a good man who himself also needs bathing and polishing. It is well now with my soul and I thank the Lord for His rebuke.

If we fall into the pattern of judging our spouse, it will only create more problems in the marriage. But accepting our spouse, and choosing to love them as they are, we will begin to see their goodness. Maybe you need to repent of judging your spouse like I needed to. Might you pray this prayer and set your marriage free to be beautiful?

Prayer of Repentance:
Lord. I have failed at being a builder of my home, and instead I have been a destroyer. Forgive me. Help us as a couple to strengthen our marriage with a humble full acceptance of one another.

Lord, I have brought my spouse hurt, rather than help in the past, and I repent of this. Because I want them to be all You want them to be, I will refrain from judging them so You can transform both of us from the inside out. I trust in Your ways and Your timing to do this. Do what You want with me to make me someone my spouse can cherish. I press into the goal of a good marriage and thank You for the beautiful union it already is. I choose to focus on You alone to satisfy all my longings so I can love my spouse as they are, imperfect but beautiful. Jesus, I surrender this all to You. Amen.

How are we to live with the imperfect spouse God has given us, and they with us? Constructively with mercy, not destructively with judgment.

CHAPTER 15

JUDGING PARENTS

The 5th commandment (Exodus 20:12) is for us to honor our mother and our father that we will have long life - a life not cut short tragically. We are to honor the two people who brought us into this world, or the people who have taken us as their own and raised us. If we are honoring our parents, we will not be judging them.

We know a good parent will do many things for their children such as provide for their needs, encourage them and train them to be responsible adults. A good parent, we will all agree, will parent with love as well as gentle discipline. We gladly honor a good parent like this, don't we? But what of the parent who parents poorly, or even abusively? Are they to be honored as well? Absolutely. The command to honor parents does not specify which kind - good or bad, near perfect or utterly imperfect. All are to be honored, abusive parents included though abuse is never acceptable. But we can still be as Christ and honor the parent who has failed at good parenting. Included in the honoring is forgiving them.

How do we honor a parent? We show them respect; we are mannerly, kind, polite and not belligerent toward them. If they were, or still are, abusive or cruel, we want them to find God and be healed; we wish them to be transformed by His love. We can choose not to hate but to pray for them. (And of course, seek safety.)

Exodus 21:17 tells us that it is wrong to curse one's father or mother. We usually think of this as a verbal damning and use of four-letter words. But remember, we produce a curse when we judge. So rather than judging, might we extend mercy to the parent, knowing there is always a reason a person is as they are. When we understand this, it will be easier for us to give the imperfect parent (all parents) grace not judgment. We do not excuse nor deny abuse and cruelty, but we seek to have Christ's compassion for them.

When I was a young woman, I would easily judge my mother. Then, in old age, my mother became feeble with dementia. She passed away just a few years back at the age of 95. But when she was feeble and needed care, I had the opportunity to periodically help with that. Seeing her so frail, I at last comprehended her preciousness and regretted judging her in my early years. They were unspoken judgments but still judgments, and I imagine she felt them. Truthfully, they were judgments over nothing of any importance. Nothing! I would not judge my mother for anything now, given another chance. I would cherish her. We only gain when we love and treasure others. When we value every human being, we are better for it.

Let us repent of all judgments we have made of a parent. Let us give them honor. Let us listen and seriously take to heart the things they share, tell them we are grateful for them, and forgive them for all their mistakes. If we honor our father and mother, and do not judge them, we will be blessed in this life!

Love values every human being.

CHAPTER 16

JUDGING SIBLINGS

The sibling relationship can be wonderful. It can also be strained, broken and painful. We can be highly compatible with a sibling or greatly challenged to relate to them. We are blessed when a sibling is also a friend.

I have two sisters and no brothers, so I don't know what goes on between brothers or between a sister and a brother. But I do know about sisters, from both experience and personal observation. I see this, that with sisters we can be way too honest with each other, saying things we would never say to a friend. We easily come right out with how we feel about things, even if we come across as insensitive. Why do we do this? Why do we take them for granted and assume they will always be there? Will they always be there? I know they can't stop being our sibling, but they sure can step out of our lives and we out of theirs. Taking offense, feeling judged and misunderstood, the sibling relationship that should be one of life's greatest blessings, can be broken and lost forever.

For us who follow Christ, taking offense is never an option. We should want to preserve our relationship with our siblings, and guard against taking and giving offense. Christ did not take offense with His siblings though He could have. When they judged Him to be out of His mind, and when they didn't believe He was the Son of God (they later came to believe), He did not take offense. And when his home town, many being relatives, did not believe in Him either, Jesus refused to be insulted by them as well. He understood that often those related to us will not honor us but judge us, and without qualm.

> *.... But Jesus said to them, "A prophet is not without honor except in his own town and in his own home."* Matthew 13:57

Even though a sibling will judge us, be excruciatingly honest with us, and be as different from us as night is from day, we should always be ready to forgive. I recently read this humorous quote: *Siblings are your only enemy you can't live without.* - unknown author. We should want to live with them, and never without them, and be willing to work at the relationship. God has given us our specific siblings. They are to be our blessing, and we theirs.

> *Siblings are your mirror, shining back at you with a world of possibilities. They are your witness, who sees you at your worst and best, and loves you anyway.* - Barbara Alpert.

Humor is always helpful. If we feel judged, let us throw in some laughter to lighten things up and heal resentments, judgments and injuries we may have with our siblings.

> *Laugh and the world laughs with you; weep, and you weep alone.*
> - Ella Wheeler Wilcox.

Taking offense is not an option if we want to preserve
our relationship with our siblings.

CHAPTER 17

REFUSING TO FORGIVE

When we refuse to forgive someone, we are judging them undeserving of love, ours as well as God's. We are declaring they are unforgivable. But is this true? Are there unforgivable people and unforgivable offenses? Jesus tells us to forgive everyone, and to forgive even 70 times repeated offenses (Matthew 18:20-22). We are to see everyone as forgivable, even the extreme cases. Jesus came to set us free. When we do not forgive someone, we will not be fully free, but be captive to our sin of unforgiveness.

There is a law about forgiveness we should consider, a law that is almost exact to the law of judging. It is this - if we refuse to forgive, we ourselves will not be forgiven – by God. In fact, we will be handed over to jailers. This is how it is put in the parable of the unmerciful servant. (See Matthew 18: 21-35). The jailers represent demonic powers that now have legal right (the door) to torment, trouble or distress us when we do not forgive. We see this when a bitter unforgiving person has lost all peace of mind because of it. We see this when someone lets their bitterness progress into hate. Mentally, they become unsound and consumed with their offender.

If we refuse to forgive someone, we stand before God in a state of unforgiveness according to Matthew 6:14-15. I want to repeat this: we will not be forgiven our offenses if we do not forgive others theirs. (Yes, the Lord will withhold His forgiveness from us.)

For if you forgive other people when they sin against you, your heavenly Father will also forgive you. But if you do not forgive others their sins, your Father will not forgive your sins. Matthew 6:14-15

What does it mean to be not forgiven by God, though we are saved, and the work of the Cross has cleansed us from all our sins? It does not mean we have lost our salvation, but it does mean that (until we forgive) we have presented the enemy opportunity to have his way with us, being outside God's full protection at the present. This is seen in the Matthew

18 parable I mentioned. However, if we will turn and forgive our offender, our sin of unforgiveness and other offenses will be forgiven; When we forgive, we close the door we opened to the enemy, and we return to the full protective covering of the Lord.

We are to forgive, but we are to also release. When we release a brother, we are saying he no longer owes us anything, even though he offended us and even though we received no apology from him. Releasing, we let go of all judgments and *punishments* we wanted him to have. Giving that person to Jesus, Jesus is now at liberty to bless the offending brother or sister, as well as us. This is drawn from the same parable, where the *unmerciful* servant was expected to *release* from prison the person who owed him something. The master in the parable expected both – forgiveness of the debt and release from imprisonment.

I find the grouping of judging, condemning and forgiveness in this verse interesting:

Do not judge, and you will not be judged. Do not condemn, and you will not be condemned. Forgive, and you will be forgiven. (Luke 6:37)

I believe these three are grouped because they are wholly linked with one another. To judge is to condemn; to not forgive is to condemn as well. And, all three actions, when we commit them, come back at us. Judging, condemning and unforgiveness are not the way of Christ. Christ called out to the Father from the Cross, asking that His Father would forgive His crucifiers and not hold it against them. In other words, do not judge nor condemn them for this. Forgive them. There were no *ifs*. He did not say, "If they ask forgiveness, forgive them Father" or, "If they feel bad about crucifying Me, then forgive them." There were no *ifs*. Should we not also follow Christ's example and forgive others without *ifs*?

Jesus said, "Father, forgive them, for they do not know what they are doing." Luke 23:34

Forgiving Self
What about forgiving self? The most troubling thing I see in regard to forgiveness is when people are unable to forgive themselves and judge themselves to be undeserving of love. They choose to live under a cloud of condemnation, and they tolerate the devil oppressing them. All

71

because they won't let go and forgive themselves. God wishes every one of His children to be free of judgment and unforgiveness, and the resulting condemnation. We can choose not only to forgive and stop judging others, but ourselves as well. If God wants to redeem our past and make beauty out of the ashes, why not let Him?

Christ has qualified us to share in all the good things of God (Colossians 1:12). Among those good things is forgiveness and the freedom that forgiveness brings. We are told to keep the law of love: to love your neighbor as yourself (Matthew 22:39). Fulfilling this law includes loving as well as forgiving ourselves. We are our own neighbor.

Won't you pray this prayer for forgiving self:

Father, because You forgive me, I will also forgive me. I release myself from all the accusations, judgments, hatred, and slander I have made against myself. I forgive myself for the mistakes, stupidity, and other ways I have fallen short of the mark. Only You, Lord, are perfect. I choose to accept myself just as I am, for You accept me as I am. I know You love me, so I choose to begin to love myself as well. I now repent of not forgiving myself, and I release myself to You to draw me onward and out of all captivity due to unforgiveness. In the name of Jesus Christ. Amen.

When we refuse to forgive someone, we are judging them to be undeserving of love, ours as well as God's.

CHAPTER 18

ASSUMING THE WORST

I marvel at those who have in them the nature to always assume the best of others. The Holy Spirit has many times convicted me of being too quick to assume the worst and negative, rather than the best and positive. How about you? Are you quick to assume the best, or the worst of a person? Have you ever, when someone failed to convey very well something with their words, jumped to a wrong conclusion and assumed they meant the worst?

Maybe you have been on the other end of this, the receiver of somebody assuming too quickly that you meant bad rather than good. When this is what happens, you can feel dishonored and misunderstood, your words butchered. This is very bothersome, and you wonder why. Why did they hear it that way and not understand what you meant? Why did they assume you would say or mean such a thing?

Assuming the worst of someone is judging them. We should seek clarity instead, and make sure we understood correctly. We can re-listen, so we don't misjudge words and ultimately, the person.

What might be some reasons we misunderstand and subsequently judge a person by their words? It might be:

1. We interpret their words according to how *we* think.
2. We have already pre-judged the person before they spoke.
3. Or, a person fails at conveying what they really mean, and we didn't seek clarification.

Let's look at some examples of assuming the worst of others:

Example 1 – Misjudging Words
There were two sisters. Each lived in a different state and their mother in a third. One sister, let's call her Trisha, wanted the other sister to travel to their mother's home for Mother's Day, as she herself intended to do. The other sister declined because she wanted to enjoy the holiday being celebrated as "mother" by her children, she said. That sounds

reasonable, doesn't it? But Trisha didn't hear it that way. In her mind she saw her sister as pampered and thinking of only herself. She judged the sister by her words, while she patted herself on the back for not being as her sister; she could sacrifice and would travel to bless their mother. These were the underlying thoughts feeding Trisha's sin of judging. She was puffed up and had no clue that she was.

Trisha's judgmental heart was exposed when she blatantly said to her sister that she didn't need gifts anymore and was willing to miss that day with her own family in order to bless their mother. Ouch! Yes, that is what she said to her sister. Sisters can be brutally honest, can't they? Imagine how her sister felt with that comment. Trisha was exalting herself, as she put her sister down.

In this example, we see Trisha has a judgmental spirit and easily assumes the worst in people – her sister anyway. She hears her sister's words negatively because she has a prejudgment of her. Trisha soon came under the conviction of the Holy Spirit and realized she was thinking herself better than her sister, judging her to be selfish and self-centered. She loved her sister, but she was not showing love to her in that moment.

Trisha apologized. When she did, her sister admitted she had indeed felt very judged by her comment; she then explained why she needed to be with her family for Mother's Day, and, it wasn't just about her. Trisha's sister graciously accepted the apology.

Because Trisha and her sister have a very open and healthy relationship, this turned out well. But what if Trisha had ignored the Holy Spirit? What if her sister had been so hurt, she would not get over it? Or, what if this was never dealt with? A breach in the sister relationship would have developed, all due to Trisha's propensity to assume the worst.

Example 2 – Misjudging Actions
In Joshua Chapter 22 we read how the people of Israel after having fought many battles, finally conquered the Promised Land (Canaan). All twelve tribes were involved in the many conquests. With the battles over, the Reubenites, Gadites, and half the tribe of Manasseh were released to go back to the other side of the Jordan where they preferred to settle. The other 9 ½ tribes settled west of the Jordan, in the Promised Land. Over time, the tribes dwelling in the Promised Land heard that the

2 ½ tribes to the east of the Jordan had built an altar. The assumption was made that the tribes to the east were committing a grave sin and had built an altar, not to the Lord, but to another god. Because of their assumption, the 9 ½ tribes readied themselves to go to war. They were willing to kill their own brothers because of an assumption.

Before Israel attacked the 2 ½ tribes to the east however, they sent a delegation with their accusations. But, their brothers to the east (Joshua 22:24-28) explained they had built the altar only as a sign to their children so they would not forget the God of Israel. The altar, a replica of the Lord's altar, was not for burnt offerings nor for other gods, but to be a witness so the Jordan River between them would not be a stumbling block in the future. They made it clear they had not committed the offense assumed of them. Thankfully the brothers living in the Promised Land received clarity about the intent of their brothers and did not go to war.

This story shows us the danger of assuming the worst, that it has the potential to destroy and kill good things, like relationships and nations. We could wonder why the 9 ½ tribes of Israel assumed the worst of their brothers after they had earlier commended them for their help in conquering their enemies. There are some possible reasons. Maybe they failed at really knowing their brothers' hearts, that they were devout men and would never do that of which they were being accused of. Or, maybe they were self-righteous, thinking themselves holier and more devout because, after all, they had settled in the Promised Land while the other tribes had not. Whatever the reasons, they judged their brothers to have the worst of intentions.

Example 3 – How it feels when the worst is assumed of us. (Names are fictitious.)

Angie: *Sometimes, I just want to relax and not clean up.*
Michelle: *Oh, I always pick up after myself. I like things clean.*

This is a very simple illustration, and one I actually heard. Put yourself in Angie's shoes. How would Michelle's comment make you feel? My guess is you would feel judged because it sounds as if Michelle assumes you are lazy or unclean. Her words, "I like things clean," are a put-down and self-righteous. Michelle is actually saying, "I am judging you to be not good."

~

I could give many more examples like that last one; examples that I have experienced myself. Words spoken so innocently but they put someone down. Imagine a world where love rules every heart, and we need never fear a wrong assumption or hurtful accusation being made against us. Just imagine! May we lose all self-righteousness and pride and put on love. Praise God we have the help of the Holy Spirit for this.

"If you judge people you have no time to love them."
Mother Teresa

I want to have time to love people.

Imagine a world where love so rules every heart that we need never fear that a wrong assumption or hurtful accusation will be made against us.

CHAPTER 19

JUDGING LAW BREAKERS

When one is given to being religious, they will judge harshly those they see breaking God's laws, though we are no longer under the law but under grace. You see, a religious person places higher importance on the *law* of the Word than the *Spirit* of the Word. The law requires perfection, while the Spirit extends love and mercy. The law says you must deserve love and earn it; the Spirit says no one can earn love, but you *are* loved. If Christ loved us while we were yet sinners and gave us divine grace, we should do the same with those breaking God's moral laws. This does not mean we encourage immorality in the church, but we deal with it with love.

Maybe you have felt the brunt of being judged by someone religious. Or, maybe you have witnessed a religious person passing judgment on someone else. And then, just maybe, it is you who judge others for not being as you (not God, but you) think they should be, with no knowledge of their journey, their story and what they came out of.

When obsessed with the dos and don'ts, we care more about the outside of a person than the inside; we disregard their heart as well as the heart of the gospel of Jesus Christ. Instead of spreading God's love, we slam a door on those we judge, refusing them admittance to the kingdom of heaven. Like the Pharisee known for his legalism, we see others beneath us because they break our laws.

> *Woe to you, teachers of the law and Pharisees, you hypocrites! You shut the door of the kingdom of heaven in people's faces. You yourselves do not enter, nor will you let those enter who are trying to.* Matthew 23:13

To the Pharisees, and to us today who judge per the law, Jesus has much to say (See Matthew 23). He calls us hypocrites and says that though we appear clean on the outside, on the inside we are not; we fail to see what we are (legalistic) and what we do to others. But God sees.

Looking at others through the lens of the law is not what the church is supposed to do. Christ does not use that lens. Having fulfilled the law, He looks through a different lens – the grace lens. Grace works in us, perfecting us through the work of sanctification by the Holy Spirit. Grace knows that we are a work in progress and justified (beyond judgment) by faith. Legalism and judgment give no space for the perfecting and the sanctifying. But love does.

For we maintain that a person is justified by faith apart from the works of the law. Romans 3:28

I came upon a book by Dave Swavely, *Who Are You to Judge?* In it I found examples of judging out of a religious spirit. They were familiar to me, having heard them many times spoken by the church and myself. You might recognize some of these statements too. Every statement below is a judgment of someone.

- There is no way someone can drive a car that expensive and be a godly man.

- A church that does not serve weekly communion is dishonoring the Lord.

- Rock music is the devil's music and is never appropriate for a Christian.

- God is sickened by the singing of simplistic praise choruses that repeat the same words over and over.

- Birth control robs God of His sovereignty and rebelliously refuses His blessings.

- Any woman who works a full-time job is neglecting her children.

- Smoking is a sin because it destroys the temple of God.

What do you think? Have you had any of these thoughts yourself? Maybe you still have them. If you do, would you think about it for a moment and ask yourself what the spirit is behind these statements? Ask yourself, "Are any of these statements supported by the scriptures?" For example, let's take that last statement – that smoking is a sin because it destroys the temple of God. The verse that is typically quoted for this argument is 1 Corinthians 6:19 that says our bodies are temples for God. That verse, however, is actually speaking to sexual morality and being pure unto the Lord; it is not speaking of the health of the physical body. Also, nowhere in the bible is smoking mentioned, nor anything like it, being a sin. Therefore, to call smoking a sin is not scriptural. It is cultural and religious. Hopefully, we can agree that God is more concerned about the heart of a man than what he puts into his body (or mouth).

The religious statements from Swavely's book are common thoughts of too many of us and I admit I have believed, and spoken, more than one of them myself. But, can you see Jesus supporting even one of those statements? I think not.

The following is taken from an article entitled, "Proclaim Not Protest" by Jack Hayford. Though he is referring to our judging the unredeemed, we can be just as harsh with those in the church who we deem not living like we think they should. Glean from these wise words:

> *"We don't gain anything by making enemies of society, by berating others for ignoring our moral standards. The Lord is calling us to manifest the heart of God for the lost, and that means we take a stance of proclamation more than protest. That doesn't mean we sacrifice our convictions or surrender to moral cowardice. But as much as I may internally protest the values of the culture, I don't perceive my call as one to protest the culture but to proclaim the Savior. Salt, if force-fed, becomes embittering. When it's sprinkled, it flavors. Light, if shined in the eyes, is blinding. But if projected into the darkness, it attracts out of the dark. It offers an answer rather than an accusation.*

Maybe we can begin today to identify religious judgments we make and repent of them, choosing to love instead. We cannot do both. We will either judge and not love, or we will not judge and love. If we love, there is gain. 1 Corinthians 13, the love chapter, tells us even if we do many things for God and think we are super spiritual people but have not love, we gain nothing. NOTHING! The remedy to this is simple if we draw from Jack Hayford's words: Stop our protesting (and judging) and instead proclaim the love of Christ.

*The definition of *religious* in this context is the imposing of strict man-made rules upon self and others to prove we are holy.

Being obsessed with the dos and don'ts of religion and caring more about the outside than the inside of a person, is to have contempt for the heart of the gospel.

CHAPTER 20

AND THESE WE ALSO JUDGE

PEERS

Judging occurs between peers when we fail at accepting and appreciating our differences. Comparing others to ourselves and finding them different than we are, we can judge them for it. We might judge one's devotion to God, comparing it to our degree of devotion. We might judge one's form of worship, also comparing it to ours. We might even judge one's personality, again, because we compare it to our own. This makes little sense, because we often rejoice that we are each made unique by God. Why then do we judge someone for their uniqueness and their being different than we are? Christ loves every one of us; He created us diverse. We ought to take delight in diversity then.

Accept one another, then, just as Christ accepted you, in order to bring praise to God. Romans 15:7

PASTORS

We are not to touch (nor condemn through the sin of judging) the Lord's anointed. We can judge their message to determine whether it is scriptural, and we can judge their life whether it is moral or not. But we are not to judge them personally. We are always to honor the men and women who God has placed in position to lead us. Our example is David's honoring King Saul. Though Saul was not a good king, a disappointment to the Lord, and though he wanted to kill David, David still respected him because of his office - king over Israel and *appointed by God* to that position. David knew that to dishonor a God-appointed leader was the same as opposing and dishonoring God Himself (1 Samuel 24:6). Because David feared God, he would not do this. We too, ought to fear God enough that we would never dishonor (and judge) a man or woman who pastors us.

Now we ask you, brothers and sisters, to acknowledge those who work hard among you, who care for you in the Lord and who admonish you. 1 Thessalonians 5:12

DENOMINATIONS

I have personally experienced a variety of denominations in my lifetime. Every one of them were a blessing to me in my season. Unfortunately, there were times, within the denomination, I heard various biases expressed against other denominations. If we take up a negative bias against other denominations, we will end up judging the people in them. When we do this, we disregard what is in the heart of the individual.

Judging denominations is sometimes heard from the pulpit. This unfortunately results in the same attitude spreading to the congregation. The Pentecostals will judge non-Pentecostals, and the non-Pentecostals will judge Pentecostals. Regarding water baptism, the sprinklers will judge the immersers, and the immersers the sprinklers. These judgments should not be. We are all of the same body – Christ's. Our focus ought to be on what unites us - Jesus Christ and His indwelling Spirit - not our disputable differences.

Let us therefore make every effort to do what leads to peace and to mutual edification. Romans 14:19

GENERATIONS

Seniors judge their juniors for not seeing things as they see them. Juniors judge their seniors for the same thing. Every generation will obviously see many things differently because every generation is unique, and each has specific experiences uniquely shaping them. This is not a bad thing, for we can reap much from past and future generations.

Generations, though diverse, are also similar. All people, of every generation, are created to know God and live for Him. Every generation consists of people who want to be loved and feel safe. They do not want to be judged, rejected, nor abused. The list goes on – the importance of family, education and health are common. We can realize that generations are actually more alike than they are different, and instead of judging different generations, we can love them and be blessed because of them.

ONE'S PLACE OF ORIGIN

It was said of Jesus' home town, "Can anything good come out of Nazareth?" Well, yes! Jesus Christ, the Messiah. Today, it might be said, "Can anything good come out of the south? Can anything good come out of the north? Can anything good come out of Mexico or Iran?" You see where I am going with this? A child of God can come out of anywhere. Let us not judge a person based on where they are born or raised. Let us instead, give them honor for their place of origin. God is a God of the nations – the cities – the villages. Let us not judge a person just because of where they come from.

TEXT MESSAGES

We can judge a person's intentions wrongly when we read a text from them. Actually, we "hear" a text when we read it. We hear an attitude, voice inflections, or the intensity of words even though there is no audio. Doing this, we might hear it as it was intended, or we might hear it different than it was intended. In that case, we then end up misjudging the text and the person. I found I was doing this with my daughter. I was hearing a voice in her texts from her younger days, before Christ changed her life, and I would sometimes have difficulty with her in my heart because of it. But one day, the Lord spoke to me about this. He stopped me as I judged her text. He said, "Is that how she is saying that? Really?" This gave me pause. I took a new look at what I was reading. I made myself read it fresh, this time hearing it from the mature woman of God she is. I was astonished. How had I missed this before? Her words were not at all as I had thought and judged them to be. I saw that her words were actually positive words. I had misjudged her. When it comes to reading texts now, I try to be very careful how I filter them. I will consider them several ways, and if it is not clear, I will ask for clarification.

~

What would you add to this chapter, that you know you judge? Maybe, you would add the judging of how others raise their children, or how they spend their money, or time. What would you include in this chapter?

Who else do you judge?

CHAPTER 21

WHEN WE <u>SHOULD</u> JUDGE

We are not prohibited from all judging. In fact, there are specific kinds of judging we are expected to do. The Word of God tells us to judge what is right and what is wrong, what is moral and what is immoral, what is truth and not truth. We do this per the Word of God which gives us the standard for what is right, moral and true. And, we do this with discernment given us by the Holy Spirit.

A teaching on acceptable judging is found in John 7. Here, Jesus directs the Pharisees to not judge by appearance but according to the heart. The Pharisees were in the habit of judging outward actions only by holding them up to the law and their church traditions. (Did the action meet the requirement of the law or abuse it?) They were not given to considering the heart of the person who was doing something that broke the law. Jesus said this was an unacceptable way to judge a man, failing to see the person acted in love, though it broke their laws.

> *Now if a boy can be circumcised on the Sabbath so that the law of Moses may not be broken, why are you angry with me for healing a man's whole body on the Sabbath? Stop judging by mere appearances, but instead judge correctly.* John 7:23-24

Another teaching on acceptable judging is 1 Corinthians 5:12 which tells us it is acceptable to judge *sin* in the church. For example, if a brother is living immorally, we are to prayerfully speak to them about it. This form of judging (judging the sin, not the brother) is for our brother's good and done to save him from wandering further from the truth. It is done also to keep the church pure, that others won't commit the same sin when they see their brother get away with it. Seeing a believer given over to sin should grieve us terribly. Therefore, when we judge (determine) someone is actually sinning, we should want to speak to them about it if we have a relationship with them. We should do this privately.

> *"If your brother or sister sins, go and point out their fault, just between the two of you. If they listen to you, you have won them over.* Matthew 18:15

A jury in a court of law determines if a crime has been committed per the legal definition of a crime. The church determines if a sin is being committed per the Word of God. I want to point out that it is the judge in a court of law who does the sentencing, not the jury. We are more as a jury than a judge in this respect. We are not the ones to condemn, give up on, nor sentence a person because of their sin. This is the sin of judging – not acceptable judging. The jury, on the other hand, looks at the crime to determine if it is a crime the person did.

Another way we can and should judge acceptably is in our evaluating all teachings of doctrine. We are to determine if a doctrine presented to us lines up with the Word of God. If it does not, we are to judge the teaching to be false and hence reject it. We can bring correction and insight to the person giving the false teaching, with gentleness of course. If all goes well, they hear us. However, if they refuse to listen and continue, we must judge them not fit for instruction in the church at this time. We put them into God's hands.

> *But even if we or an angel from heaven should preach a gospel other than the one we preached to you, let them be under God's curse! As we have already said, so now I say again: If anybody is preaching to you a gospel other than what you accepted, let them be under God's curse!* Galatians 1:8, 9

It is also acceptable for us to judge spirits and determine whether the spirit speaking through a man (prophet, preacher, teacher) is of God or not. One may prophesy, preach or teach out of their own flesh, or by the inspiration of the enemy. We are to test every spirit, as it is put in 1 John.

> *Dear friends, do not believe every spirit, but test the spirits to see whether they are from God, because many false prophets have gone out into the world.* 1 John 4:1

Testing the spirits is for gaining discernment. Sometimes we can be overly cautious not wanting to judge others and will confuse the gift of discernment with the sin of judging. To avoid making this mistake, we need to understand the difference between the two. I have an example that may help. This is Joanne's story. (The names have been changed.)

Years ago, my husband and I had befriended a man who was one of those hard-to-love Christians. He had some character flaws – he boasted in himself a lot, he lacked discipline and he talked on and on. My husband was always one to reach out to the underdog, and so we reached out to this man, inviting him into our home often. We wanted to love him as Christ loved him. However, we struggled with this. We would reprimand ourselves for having negative feelings toward the man. Though he was highly unlovable, we felt we should love him and accept him. We'd pray for love – a good feeling in our heart toward this man, but it wouldn't come. But we continued to embrace this man, had him in our home often, and even let him watch our toddler daughter a few times. We eventually moved away and lost touch with him. After a few short years, some facts came out about this man and brought to our attention. He had been arrested, along with others, for meeting in a public park and committing sexually perverse acts. My husband gave him a call and confronted him with this. He hemmed and hawed but eventually admitted it. But he wasn't repentant at all, only casting blame on others. We realized something then. We realized we weren't judging this man in the past; we were getting discernment. The Lord had been trying to protect our daughter and our home from a perverse spirit this man harbored and didn't want to be delivered from. In the past, we didn't understand the difference between the sin of judging and discernment. Today, we have greater wisdom. We now know, if we pray to have a good feeling toward someone, which we thought was feeling love, and it doesn't come, it is God's protection and discernment.

I hope this has been clear for you, that we can sense something is not right about someone, and it is not that we are judging them. Discernment reveals a spirit and warns us when there is evil present. If the one given to evil is not repentant but wishes to remain in their sin and house an evil spirit, it is okay to step back from them. We are not judging but being wise. We are to know and discern, what is in the tree, by the fruit.

Acceptable judging is the discerning and determining between right and wrong, moral and immoral, truth and lies.

CHAPTER 22

SELF-EXAMINATION

Some honest self-examination is always good for determining whether we might be judging someone at present or if we have in the past. If we are or have, we will want to repent, so we can move forward into victory over this sin. Following are some questions to ask yourself in order to discern how your heart is toward others, and whether you are judging them. I suggest reading this chapter first, then answer the questions. (They are repeated at the end.) The questions:

- <u>Who </u>rubs you the wrong way?
- <u>Why</u> do they rub you the wrong way?

- <u>Who </u>do you have difficulty loving, or even liking?
- <u>Why</u> do you have difficulty loving them?

- <u>Who </u>do you not accept but reject?
- <u>Why </u>can you not accept them?

After each set of questions, ask, "What do you say about this Lord?" Here are some examples:

Example 1

Who rubs me wrong? Jane Smith.

Why? Jane is a braggart, and I find her intolerable to be with because of this.

What do you say about this, Lord? You are judging. You are rejecting Jane unworthy of your love based on her sin of bragging. Child, you are not separating the sin from the sinner. Separate them and you will love the sinner. You do not know why she brags, and you have not considered her heart in this. Jane needs your love, not your judgment. Might you be the one to befriend her in spite of her bragging, and show her Me.

Note: To say Jane brags is fact. But to call her a braggart is judging. Jane is more than her sin. Judging has no concern for Jane to grow and become more like Christ. But love and concern will pray for Jane and help her when given the opportunity. We don't have to be Jane's best friend, but we do have to care about her. And we should never label (define) anyone by their sin. This condemns them. They are children of God or one day may be, and Jesus wishes them to have life abundantly.

Your prayer: Lord, forgive me for judging Jane Smith by defining her as a braggart. I forgive myself for making this judgment. I remove all legal rights and power I gave the enemy to carry out this judgment. I release God's freedom and healing to Jane Smith, that she would become so secure in Your love she would not need to brag. Help me to love her as she is, Lord. Amen.

Example 2
Who do I have difficulty loving? John Doe.

Why? He is inaccurate with the Word of God when he teaches. He is unacceptable to me as a teacher.

Lord, what do you say about this? It may be true that John has some growing to do in the Word, and maybe he isn't ready to teach yet. But, on the other hand, John is stepping up to serve Me, and I wish to train him in this area. It is okay to judge the teaching, but you should not be condemning him when he errs. John can be taught, and I know he will listen if you speak with him. Pray for John and you will see him making less errors. John could end up being a very good teacher unless condemnation from others causes him to give up.

Your Prayer: Lord, I ask forgiveness for judging John Doe so harshly. I judged him for not being perfect, and I wrote him off. I forgive myself for making this judgment. I now remove all legal rights and power I gave to the demonic to carry out this judgment. I release God's freedom and healing to John Doe, and I bless him with wisdom and an accurate handling of God's Word. Amen.

Doesn't it feel so much better to bless, rather than judge?

Example 3
Who do I not accept but reject? Martha Doe.

Why? She always cancels out on our plans together. She is flakey. I just can't deal with being treated like that. I'm done with her.

Lord, what do you say about this? Child, Martha is not flaky. She has good reason every time she cancels. She has many grandchildren, and they are her ministry. She is doing my will. Give her grace.

Your prayer: Forgive me Lord, for my judgment against <u>Martha,</u> that she is flakey. I forgive myself for this judgment. I now remove all legal rights and power I gave to the demonic spirits to carry out my judgment. I release God's freedom and healing to <u>Martha,</u> that she would be blessed in all she does. Amen.

Note: Martha had committed no sin, but the judgment was that she had.

In all these examples, the sin of judging was present. But I want to give one more example, where judging was not the case. Let's use the last set of questions.

Example 4

Who do I not accept but reject? The man down the street.

Why? I saw him beating a dog. He is violent, dangerous, and even evil. He is bad; I don't want to be around him. I get chills when I see him.

Lord, what do you say about this? This is not judging, My child. You witnessed a man given over to evil spirits. He is dangerous and I want you to be careful. You did not judge him; you discerned danger. I will use others to redeem him. You can reject being near this man but *accept* him redeemable and pray for him.

YOUR TURN

I hope these examples have helped clarify what judging looks like. Now, get a pen and write down your answers to the questions. Remember to ask the Lord if you are judging and listen to what He says about it. If you find that you are judging, release the person from the judgment and repent of your sin. May God bless your self-examination as you submit to the guidance of the Holy Spirit.

Father, help me in my self-examination. Speak to me that I can know how you see things. Amen.

Question 1
- Who rubs you the wrong way?

- Why do they rub you the wrong way?

- Father, what do you say about this?

Question 2
- Who do you have difficulty loving, or even liking?

- Why can't you love them?

- Father, what do you say about this?

Question 3
- Who do you not accept but reject?

- Why is it you don't accept them?

- Father, what do you say about this?

Are you in need of repentance? Will you say this prayer?

PRAYER

I ask You to forgive me, Lord, for my judgment of _____ that they are_____. I forgive myself for this judgment. I now remove all legal rights and power I gave to the demonic spirits to carry out this judgment. I release God's freedom and healing to _____ (the person you judged). Lord, bless them to _____. Amen.

Create in me a clean heart, Lord.
Psalm 51:10

CHAPTER 23

FILLED WITH HIS-ATTITUDES

Now that we are getting rid of the judgmental spirit we've had and tolerated for too long, with what shall we fill the emptied space? How about some godly attitude? We find eight of them in Jesus' Sermon on the Mount, where he taught the beatitudes to His disciples (Matthew 5:3-10). When filled with these attitudes, we are promised to be blessed. And blessed, we will be a blessing to others.

AN ATTITUDE OF HUMILITY
BLESSED ARE THE POOR IN SPIRIT
If we come to realize how poor in spirit we truly are, that we are sinners in need of forgiveness and mercy, then we will have the attitude of humility. Let us be *filled* then, with the knowledge of our depravity outside of God, so we will be merciful to others and not judge them. After all, who are we to judge any brother when we are poor in spirit ourselves? *Lord, please fill me with the knowledge of my poverty so my attitude will be one of humility.*

AN ATTITUDE OF COMPASSION
BLESSED ARE THOSE WHO MOURN
Rather than judging a brother, let us grieve and mourn over his shortcomings, failures, and imperfections. Let us grieve and mourn so much that we will be filled with compassion, compelled to pray for him. *Lord, fill me with mourning regarding my brother's troubles, that my attitude will be one of compassion.*

AN ATTITUDE OF MEEKNESS
BLESSED ARE THE MEEK
If meek, we will let go and let God work in our brother and sister. We will believe in His ability to transform and deliver them. If we fail at being meek, we get in God's way and judge. *Lord, fill me with an attitude of meekness so I will let go and trust in Your ways and Your timing to work in others.*

AN ATTITUDE OF REPENTANCE
BLESSED ARE THOSE WHO HUNGER AND THIRST FOR RIGHTEOUSNESS

To hunger and thirst for righteousness is to be concerned whether it is found in ourselves and to repent of all our own unrighteousness. We are not to be consumed with the righteousness (or unrighteousness) of others, which only results in our judging them. But we examine ourselves only and repent when needed. *Lord, fill me with a hunger and thirst for Your ways, that my attitude will be one of repentance for all sins and judgments I commit.*

AN ATTITUDE OF MERCY
BLESSED ARE THE MERCIFUL

The merciful forgive and allow others to be human and make mistakes. If merciful, we extend love to the one who falters and fails. We release a brother of all his offenses and never hold a grudge or judgment against him. And the merciful person is thankful for God's mercy toward them. *Lord, fill me with Your attitude of mercy.*

AN ATTITUDE OF GRACE
BLESSED ARE THE PURE IN HEART

When we have a pure heart, we see the best, hope for the best, and pray for the best for others. With a pure heart, there is no evil intent, no judgment. Instead, we extend abundant grace, love, and favor without it being earned. *Lord, fill me with an attitude of grace toward my brother.*

AN ATTITUDE OF ENCOURAGEMENT
BLESSED ARE THE PEACEMAKERS

As a peacemaker, we will be affirming and wish others to succeed. We will always be for and never against a brother. A peacemaker does not judge, for judging disturbs peace. First and foremost, we will want our brother to be right with God and will encourage him to be so. *Lord, fill me with an attitude of encouragement.*

AN ATTITUDE OF ENDURANCE
BLESSED ARE WE WHEN PERSECUTED BECAUSE OF RIGHTEOUNESS

May we be willing to stand up for righteousness and always do what is righteous, even when it costs us. Though others may complain, slander or judge, may we not join with them. Instead, with an attitude to endure in righteousness, let us stand firm, always looking to God. *Lord, fill me with the attitude of endurance that I will persevere in doing all that is good and righteous in Your eyes, even if I am persecuted for it.*

~

Is there an attitude, other than these eight, that could transform how we relate with people, and dissuade us from judging others? May we seek to be filled with the attitudes of God!

PRAYER
Lord fill me, Your temple, with Your glory and Your Spirit. Remind me of my poverty, grant me compassion for a brother in trouble, and teach me the way of meekness so I will trust You to work in my bother. Transform my heart, make it pure and full of grace. Help me see how I can affirm and encourage others. Strengthen me, that I will continue in all your ways, always choosing righteousness. Amen.

You were taught . . . . to be made new in the attitude of your minds; and to put on the new self, created to be like God in true righteousness and holiness. Ephesians 4:22-24

CHAPTER 24

A CONFESSION - MINE

This I know - when I judge, it is out of pride; when I judge, God will humble me. I know that I am a work in progress because I still deal with pride, and I still judge. God is humbling me daily, and I understand Paul full well when he said:

For I do not do the good I want to do, but the evil I do not want to do—this I keep on doing. Now if I do what I do not want to do, it is no longer I who do it, but it is sin living in me that does it.

So I find this law at work: Although I want to do good, evil is right there with me. For in my inner being I delight in God's law; but I see another law at work in me, waging war against the law of my mind and making me a prisoner of the law of sin at work within me. What a wretched man I am! Who will rescue me from this body that is subject to death? Thanks be to God, who delivers me through Jesus Christ our Lord! Romans 7:19-25

So, the other night, because I am still a work in progress, this is what came out of my mouth and directly from my heart of pride - a heart I so want to be a heart of humility but isn't – yet. This is the story:

My husband and I had been binging on a television series that we both enjoyed. After viewing a few episodes, we would normally have some good discussion, trying to figure out the direction of the plot. This night, after viewing several new episodes, my husband headed to bed, and I stepped outside where I viewed a beautiful array of stars in the expansive sky. God's handiwork amazed me; it was so beautiful. I had not taken time to marvel at God's creation for some time, and it was truly remarkable to observe. But the devil got into the moment for I then reprimanded myself, "This is where my wonder and thoughts should be. Not on a fictional television story." I soon went in the house to go to bed myself, but my thoughts were whirling, and I kept scolding myself for those hours of watching television with my husband. The fact is my husband loves television more than I do, but we bond when we find a program that we both like; it is good for our marriage that we have something to share.

But that fact didn't matter to me in the moment, and I began to judge (cast the blame on) myself, and then on him, for not contemplating on God enough. In my mind, I soon made it all his fault that I wasn't as I should be. (A religious spirit was definitely at work in me.) And so, I went to bed, where I found him still awake. This is where I opened my big mouth. "Honey," I said, "you need to be spending more time thinking about God, not this television show." (Not a we, but a you, mind you.)

I was all sweet when I said this. But the moment I had spoken, it felt so so wrong. Ugh. I immediately realized I had just released a horrible spirit. However, I went to sleep and left it at that. All night I dreamed; I dreamed of the characters in the series we had watched. All night they were in my dreams, instead of God dreams like I sometimes have. Morning came. I awoke and got in the shower, where God immediately spoke to me, showing me what I had actually done the night before - I had judged my husband and he had done nothing wrong. NOTHING! I had been self-righteous. And I had laid my expectations for myself upon him. Lord, have mercy! And what was the result of my judging him? I did that which I judged him for – thinking on the series excessively all through the night. I had to repent and ask forgiveness. I was humbled by the conviction of the Holy Spirit and shown I am no different than my husband, except that I am self-righteous, and he is not. And I was shown I still judge.

When a heart is filled with pride, it will be a judge; a humble heart will not. I want to do what is right; I want to be humble and not proud. But acquiring a humble heart is a process. I know God is determined to complete this in me, and He will eventually accomplish it. In that process, I thank God that….

When pride comes, then comes disgrace, but with humility comes wisdom. Proverbs 11:2

It may take a lifetime before I do not judge anyone ever again. But I know this - I judge less than I used to and for that, I give God praise. I give Him praise that He loves me as I am, and that He and I together are working on my heart - which desires to please Him more each day. Regardless of my condition, I am His and He is mine; He comes into my

102

garden and He enjoys me. The maiden, in the Song of Songs, echoes my heart:

> *My beloved has gone down to his garden, to the beds of spices, to browse in the gardens and to gather lilies. I am my beloved's and my beloved is mine; he browses among the lilies.* Song of Songs 6:2-3

My prayer:
Lord, I ask that You keep working on my heart of pride, bringing me to a lower place than I was yesterday, a humbler place. I wish death to all my self-righteousness. I am grateful for Your love, and my husband's love. Thank You Lord, for Your faithfulness to me. Amen.

CHAPTER 25

AN ALLEGORY

Free-Will, America

On a sometimes (and sometimes not) pleasant street, oddly named People's Court, live two families who we shall now acquaint ourselves with. In the two-story brick house on the corner is the Grace family. Mr. Grace, Love is his first name, runs a factory, Olive-Branch, Inc., where he and 12 employees produce t-shirts, jewelry, banners, table cloths – you name it – everything under the sun and all bearing the olive branch. Love enjoys explaining the meaning of the olive branch, that it is historically and biblically a symbol of peace and good will. Mrs. Grace, Mercy is her first name, is a nurse who cares for the elderly. From the union of Love and Mercy, have come two exceptionally kindhearted daughters - Acceptance and Encouragement.

Four houses down from the Graces live the Laws. Mr. Law is the local judge and has been for a very long time. His name is Self-Righteous, a name fondly given him by his father, Pharisee. His wife is Pride, a pretty and petite woman but with a strong way about her. Pride takes fancy in making things beautiful – her garden, her home, her children and herself. Self-Righteous and Pride have a daughter, Critical, and a son, Assume. Critical has won many prizes and trophies for being exceptional at seeing others' faults and calling them out. She never lets a fault go undetected and is an expert at measuring others up, categorizing them as this or that. Assume is proficient at assuming all kinds of things about people based on nothing more than his own hasty observations. This gift flows quite naturally for Assume, who inherited the skill from his maternal grandmother, Quick-to-Judge.

The Graces and the Laws live in the town of Free-Will and have lived there all their lives. Both attend the neighborhood church just two blocks north of their homes. The church is situated right across the street from the *Stay-the-Same Amusement Park* that has a very popular merry-go-round. And down the street, just a little way further, is the *Humble Pie Restaurant* and the *Get-Clean Laundromat*. Church attenders frequent these three places often, usually right after church. When they don't dine or cleanse, it is because they have chosen to visit the amusement park and ride the merry-go-round, going in circles and getting nowhere new. This seems pointless to those who go to *Humble Pie Restaurant* or *Get-Clean Laundromat.*

The church the Graces and Laws attend has the distinguished name First Free-Will Church of Love. Pastor Forgiveness leads the sixty-soul congregation. Yearly, these fine people put together a tasty chicken-fry dinner in the fall and a much anticipated craft bazaar in the spring. They are known for the tall bell steeple that chimes *Amazing Grace* every Sunday morning at 9:00 a.m.

But we have a story to tell that happened there in Free-Will, America, on People's Court, which is a normal street in a normal town of normal people. As the story goes, one day in early October when the trees were at their peak of color and autumn leaves crunched underfoot, the Law children were outdoors playing a game of Tag-Run-and-Scream. They paused in their play, however, when they came upon a man sitting on the curb in front of their grand, three-story house built of chaff. (Quite a tourist attraction for those visiting Free-Will.) Anyway, the Law children, Critical and Assume, did not know this man and were confident it was their job to observe and form an opinion of him. Why this man sat there on the curb was a mystery, but the why wasn't so important to them. No, they had other ways to approach such a mystery, and it was to assume. Assume took the lead in this (no surprise there), and assumed the man was casing out their home to burgle it. He also assumed the man homeless and undesirable. And with his sister, he assumed the stranger was not only trouble, but far below them in pedigree. After all, they were the children of Self-Righteous and Pride Law, distinguished citizens of Free-Will.

Soon Critical and Assume ventured a bit closer to the man and took up conversation with him. That was when Critical called upon her gift of criticizing. In her heart she was critical of the man's speech. He had an accent of some sort because he sure didn't talk like her when he greeted them. Because of this, she determined he must be unintelligent. (In her mind, a strange accent was a sure sign of not being very bright.) Then she criticized him, out loud now, regarding his manner of dress. His clothes were soiled and nothing similar to her father's fine black robes of justice. She snuffed at his boniness and judged him lazy for sitting there on the curb and not working somewhere, like her father.

After Critical and Assume gave the man the fullness of their gifts (for that is what they thought them to be), they went into their house where they quickly disclosed to their father all their assumptions and criticisms of the man sitting at the curb. Self-Righteous agreed that this man was up to no good. He patted himself on the back for having put in a full day in court, having gone in at 10:00 a.m. and then finishing at 1:00 p.m. A full day, indeed, of judging people just like that man there at the curb.

Now, when Pride Law joined them at the window to stare at this stranger, she instantly judged and agreed the man to be of low appeal, uneducated, and possessing no drive to make something of himself. "Just look at how he holds his head, and that unshaved face," she said. "Not beautiful at all," she added.

The Laws left their window and proceeded to go about whatever they normally do. Meanwhile, the Graces came home, driving by this man at the curb. Mother (Mercy) noticed the gentleman first and had Father, always full of love, stop the car. Mercy got out, questioned the man a bit, then invited him into their car to go home with them and have dinner, a shower and, of course, a comfortable bed. And that is what happened. The man, (they discovered his name was Mis-Judged), graciously accepted their offer and soon found himself at the dinner table to a meal of Beef Wellington, mashed potatoes and a huge mound of green beans from Mercy's garden. As they dined and talked, they discovered Mis-Judged to be a very interesting man. They heard his story of being robbed of his money and all identification in the large city some 30 miles down the road. Because of the robbery, he was destitute and trying desperately to get home; he had walked for hours. They also learned that he was a professor at a seminary in another state, teaching mainly on the Fruit of the Spirit. His clothes were soiled because he had just finished helping a chimney sweep that morning, earning a few dollars enough for lunch and a phone call to a friend. The friend was in route right now to pick him up and take him home – a good six-hour drive. He explained that it had been a rough day, his only help coming from the chimney sweep, and now, them. How did he happen upon their street? A good shade tree had drawn him there to wait for his ride, hours off. "The silver lining in all of this," he said, "is my meeting the Graces!"

The Graces continued to discover more about Mis-Judged and his deep faith. They saw he was of good character, gracious, loving, and forgiving. A friendship formed between them that evening. Mis-Judged was delighted with the spirit of Acceptance and cheered by the words of Encouragement. They all enjoyed a delightful time.

Around 9:00 p.m. the friend of Mis-Judged, Servant, who had received a second phone call, now from the Graces, showed up at the door. Another friendship was formed, and both men were given a bed for the night, with their plans to leave the next day, Sunday.

The next morning, Mis-Judged and his friend, Servant, were happy to attend church with the Graces before they would head home. After church, and on their way to *Humble Pie Restaurant*, they passed the *Stay-the-Same Amusement Park*. Enjoying a good conversation, they didn't see the Laws standing in line at the merry-go-round having some trouble. The talk in town was the ticket man, a new man on the job, judged the Laws to be people of low pedigree. He also made the quick assumption they were trying to sneak in without purchasing tickets, for they couldn't produce any. He had no clue this was Judge Self-Righteous and his family and so he turned them away.

That is the story, but the good part of it is, that over the years the friendship between the Graces and Mis-Judged continued. The Graces kept on loving, accepting, and showing mercy towards others, and they reaped many new and beautiful friendships.

May we be known for having
mercy and love!

CHAPTER 26

A BLESSING

I BLESS YOU, my reader, to be an imitator of God, living a life of love.

I BLESS YOU to be a sweet aroma of Christ to your brother because you will not judge him, but accept, forgive and love him.

I BLESS YOU to be, not a hindrance nor a stumbling block to others, but a blessing and source of encouragement.

I BLESS YOU to be one who always calls upon the Lord to assist those you see are having struggles, holding them up to the throne of God, praying they succeed and prosper.

I BLESS YOU to be free from the weight of judgments others have made of you, and that you can have the grace to love those who do not love you as they should.

I BLESS YOU to always refrain from comparing yourself to others, and others to yourself.

I BLESS YOU to be free from condemning, rejecting and sizing others up.

I BLESS YOU to be known as a person of mercy and love, kindness and compassion.

In Christ all things are possible. Amen.

JUDGE NOT

~

EVER

DID YOU KNOW?

Judgements prevent us from seeing the good that lies beyond
appearances. ~ Wayne Dyer

Everyone may not be good, but there's always something good
in everyone. Never judge anyone shortly because every saint has
a past, and every sinner has a future. ~ Oscar Wilde

The more rules you have about how people have to be,
how life has to be for you to be happy, the less happy
you're going to be. ~ Tony Robbins

Hesitancy in judgment is the only true
mark of the thinker. ~ Dagobert D. Runes

OTHER BOOKS BY PATSY SCOTT

BETWEEN PORCH AND ALTAR: Intercessory Prayers and Teaching for the Prayer Closet.

QUESTIONS JESUS ASKED: A 25-day devotional to stir your spirit and fine-tune your spiritual ears.

MAKE ME A HOUSE OF PRAYER: Devotions and meditations for a 21-day fast.

A HOUSE OF PRAYER: Powering up –Sweeping out – Surrendering: 21 days of Meditation and Prayer. (Same book as the above but without fasting references).

THE BOOK OF RUTH: A Bible Study for Small Groups and Individuals.

THE POWER OF LOVE: 8 Bible-Based Lessons for Individual or Group Study.

THE POWER TO STAND FIRM: 8 Bible-Based Lessons for Individual or Group Study.

THE POWER OF CONSECRATION: 7 Bible-Based Lessons for Individual or Group Study.

THE POWER OF KNOWING: 8 Bible-Based Lessons for Individual or Group Study.

JAMES: Living a Blessed Life. A Bible Study on the Book of James.

GOD IN US: How we ought to live. A primer for living as we should.

These books may be found on www.amazon.com.

DANCING WITH JESUS: Intimate poetry – Intimate God

This book can be purchased on www.barnesandnoble.com

Made in the USA
Middletown, DE
20 November 2021